Coleridge, Language, and Criticism

Coleridge, Language, and Criticism

TIMOTHY CORRIGAN

The University of Georgia Press
Athens

Copyright © 1982 by the University of Georgia Press
Athens, Georgia 30602
All rights reserved

Set in 10 on 13 Trump Mediaeval
Printed in the United States of America
Designed by Francisca Vassy

Library of Congress Cataloging in Publication Data

Corrigan, Timothy.
Coleridge, language, and criticism.

Bibliography: p.
Includes index.
1. Coleridge, Samuel Taylor, 1772–1834—
Knowledge.   2. Coleridge, Samuel Taylor,
1772–1834—Style.
I. Title.
PR4483.C596 1982   821'.7   81-10433
ISBN 0-8203-0593-6   AACR2

For Lore Metzger and Frank O'Malley

We learn words by rote but not their meaning;
that must be paid for with our life-blood, and
printed in the subtler fibres of our nerves.
GEORGE ELIOT,
The Lifted Veil

Contents

Acknowledgments

Two CHAPTERS OF THIS STUDY originally appeared in slightly modified forms as separate essays: Chapter 1 in *Philological Quarterly* (Winter 1979) and chapter 4 in *Journal of the History of Ideas* (Summer 1980). I am grateful to both publications for permission to incorporate these articles into this larger work.

More specifically, there are a number of friends and colleagues who have played a large part in the writing and the completion of this study, all of whom deserve far more thanks than these few lines can offer. At the University of Notre Dame, Joseph Duffy, William Krier, Thomas Jemielity, John McDonald, and Frank O'Malley have each in their very different ways been long-standing motivating forces. Professors Marilyn Gaull, Alan Wilde, George McFadden, Susan Stewart, and many others at Temple University have, during the last stages of the book, provided an extremely helpful forum within which to discuss some of the theoretical issues raised here. From Professor J. Robert Barth, the manuscript gained considerably; his criticisms were consistently on the mark and more than sympathetic.

At Emory University, Jerome Beaty led me to some of the original questions behind this study, and he continued to offer valuable advice at many points along the way. Also at Emory, David Cook has been such a pervasive influence on my work and thinking in so many capacities, that this acknowledgment is especially inadequate. Lore Metzger likewise deserves much more thanks than is appropriate here; particular points and conclusions are not necessarily her own, but the spirit of inquiry is a product of my fortunate contact with her as a scholar and a friend. She directed the research for this book with extraordinary patience, energy, and flexibility, and, as a true Coleridgean, she read the manuscript with sympathy, rigor, and imagination.

Finally, I would like to thank Mark Richardson, Kay Smith, Scott Wilson, and particularly Kathy King, who taught me that even the fine lines must go sometimes; Marcia Ferguson and her family for some perspective and several new words; and my parents and brothers, not only for their unquestioning support but also for their marvelous diversity.

Coleridge, Language, and Criticism

Introduction

THAT LITERARY CRITICISM HAS DEVELOPED in so many new directions in the last two decades while at the same time interest in Coleridge's writings grows proportionately is more than coincidental. What some of the most penetrating and imaginative writers of the nineteenth and twentieth centuries realized—writers like J. S. Mill and Kenneth Burke—becomes increasingly apparent today as literary theorists and critics test new avenues into literature and art: namely, however inconsistent and opaque Coleridge's literary criticism and theory is at times, it demonstrates an unprecedented scope, flexibility, and almost prophetic sensitivity to the complexities and nuances of literature. Celebrated for so long as a great aesthetic idealist and champion of the imagination, Coleridge has begun to be understood as a literary critic with many other dimensions, with exciting and far-reaching insights into language, and with detailed notions about the psychological, historical, and linguistic demands of the literary experience.

Without discounting those traditional perspectives on Coleridge, this study accordingly proposes a different point of view, one that examines Coleridge's literary criticism as the product of an actively self-conscious reader, of a precise user of language, and, most of all, of a historical man involved with the demands of his day. Undoubtedly this emphasis is aligned with a great deal of work now being done in reader-response theory and in structuralist linguistics. Yet, referring to these contemporary methodologies as guiding ideas for an investigation of Coleridge's literary criticism indicates only that his work is not a closed and strictly defined system, but rather an extraordinarily diverse practice that responds sympathetically to new angles of research.

The questions behind my approach to Coleridge therefore draw consciously on the work of many contemporary theorists like Roland Barthes, Jonathan Culler, and Julia Kristeva, besides older critics like Roman Ingarden and R. S. Crane. More specifically, using some of the ideas of these writers as a backdrop, my argument takes its particular direction from the concepts of naturalization and intertextuality, as defined by structuralist critics and as operative in Coleridge's prose. This naturalization process is, in brief, the act by which an otherwise distant literary text is assimilated and understood in terms of the reader's own historical and cultural formulas: in Culler's words, "The strange, the formal, the fictional, must be recuperated or naturalized, brought within our ken, if we do not want to remain gaping before monumental inscriptions, . . . for to assimilate or interpret something is to bring it within the modes of order which culture takes as natural."[1] In my analysis, these modes of order become the codes for interpretation in Coleridge's reading and criticism, codes which can be isolated in terms of certain historical periods in which interests like politics or science markedly control Coleridge's interpretations of literature.

Seen as a coding process, naturalization is thus the foundation for the notion of intertextuality, whereby the significance of a literary text, for example, is the product of its relation to other extraliterary texts such as those of theology, politics, or science. A text resonates with meanings not explicitly in it but attached to the historical and cultural languages surrounding it. Or, as Culler explains,

> The best way of imagining a relationship between literature and society which could form the basis of cultural

history and hence literary history is to think of both literature and the culture of which it forms a part as institutions composed of semiological systems. Culture itself is a set of symbolic systems which enable actions or objects to have meaning, and among these systems is that of literature, or of the various literary genres, whose conventions are devices for the production and organization of meaning. By thinking of literature and culture in this way, as systems of signs, we produce a relationship of commensurability: it becomes possible to use a common vocabulary in discussing them, and in bringing the two together we establish an integrating principle which can serve as the basis of a common historical series. We make possible a history of the conventions for the production of meaning which are deployed in the literature and the culture of the period.

One might put this claim another way by saying that the relationship between literature and society is not one of identity or content but of homology of form.[2]

In suggesting this perspective on Coleridge's critical texts and reading practices, I am obviously moving the focus from the primary text—the poem or novel the structuralists almost always examine—which generates meaning, to the critical work, which produces meaning. The theoretical mechanics are, however, much the same in either case; particularly helpful in terms of the critical text are Derrida's notion of "supplementarity," whereby one sign can always substitute for and supplement another as a critical sign supplements a poetic sign, and Barthes's connotative text, where a word or phrase releases "the double meaning on principle, corrupts the purity of communication."[3] Doubtless these ideas are not as revolutionary or original as some believe, yet their distinctly linguistic emphasis and description of cultures and history itself as sign systems makes them valuable

starting points for an investigation of the interaction of Coleridge's critical texts and his extraliterary interests.

As with any sort of critical practice, this slant on Coleridge's writings admits certain limitations. Segmenting Coleridge's intellectual life into discrete historical units is, for
instance, a sin against the spirit of his life and the vitality of
his mind. If Coleridge participated in many different kinds of
knowledge, from the scientist's to the theologian's, he clearly
united them in the singularity of his great vision. As a critic
and reader of literature, Coleridge may have read in the languages of the politician and the psychologist, yet the complementary poet in him merged these different tongues into
a truly harmonious tower of Babel. A poet as well as a critic,
Coleridge always sought "the identity of all other knowledge" and all other languages, since "a poet cannot be a great
poet but by being likewise and inclusively an historian and
naturalist. . . . All other men's words . . . are *his* chaos."[4]

Yet this schematizing of Coleridge's critical opus is prob-
lematic for still another, more challenging reason: namely, it
ignores the confluence of different areas of knowledge and
different languages through the course of personal and historical development. Quite obviously, Coleridge never used
one "language" exclusively for a period of a few years, just as
he never pursued one area of knowledge for a period of time
only to switch his allegiance to another discipline a few
years later. Political codes, political interests, and political
rhetoric follow Coleridge throughout his life, as do psychological codes and biological interests. For the purpose of my
argument, I have had to isolate specific blocks of time in
Coleridge's life, and examine the languages and interests
that predominated in these blocks as if they were separate
paradigmatic units. This however has been one of those
minor fictions needed for argumentation, since in fact these
units of time infiltrate each other, dirty the purity of each
other's communication, and grow off each other as they in-

4

variably assimilate each other. The truth is that Coleridge's theological language is permeated by the history of his political and scientific language, and what were originally psychological terms are often the root words for the lexicons that come later in Coleridge's life. In structuralist jargon what this means is that I have chosen to concentrate on the synchronic dimensions of Coleridge's reading and criticism, and willfully to underplay the diachronic fluidity of his reading and writing.

A final limitation to my approach is that, like Coleridge's criticism itself, my argument often becomes dependent on the terminology of its source. Expressions such as *naturalization* or *actualize* are not overly troublesome since these are quite familiar to Romantic criticism, especially that concerned with Coleridge. Other trendier expressions such as *code* do, however, appear occasionally since often no suitable substitute can be found to suggest succinctly the process by which the reader's language transforms and translates meaning. Yet, on the whole, I have tried to avoid jargon just as I have avoided any kind of equation between Coleridge and contemporary theorists. This study is first and foremost an investigation of Coleridge's criticism based on Coleridge's own ideas about language and reading. If there is a coincidence of ideas across two centuries, this should above all redound to Coleridge's credit. If contemporary theories of language and literature open new avenues into Coleridge's criticism as their terminology pinpoints new issues, this is not because they autonomously create those avenues but because they shed new light on a writer and thinker who consistently resists any one perspective and whose diversity will always be a rich fund for many points of view.

CHAPTER ONE

Coleridge, the Reader:
Language in a Combustible Mind

*But how are we to guard against the herd of
promiscuous Readers? . . . The event lies
with the Reader.*
RUDOLF VON LANGEN

*In reading we must become aware of what we
write unconsciously in our reading.*
PHILIPE SOLLERS,
Logiques

SCATTERED THROUGHOUT COLERIDGE'S NOTES AND ESSAYS is an oblique but relentless fight with a "much-reading, but not very hard-reading age."[1] More specifically, he attacks a large group of not-so-gentle readers whose lazy and careless methods spawn so much mindless literary criticism and whose failure to react to literature with sensitivity and imagination creates not only an ebb in the quality of literary criticism but in the quality of the entire culture as well. The quotation above from Rudolf von Langen, for instance, begins an early essay in *The Friend*, "On the Communication of Truth," and the passage goes on to illustrate what a powerful part the reader plays in determining the meaing of a text, and, furthermore, how easily he misuses that power. Von Langen continues,

> I purchased lately Cicero's work, de officiis, which I had always considered as almost worthy a Christian. To my surprize it had become a most flagrant libel. Nay! but how?—Some one, I know not who, out of the fruitfulness of his own malignity had filled all the margins and other blank spaces with annotations—a true *superfoetation* of *examples*, that is, of false and slanderous tales! In like manner, the slave of impure desires will turn the pages of Cato, not to say, Scripture itself, into occasions and excitements of wanton imaginations. There is no wind but feeds a volcano, no work but feeds and fans a combustible mind.[2]

For von Langen and Coleridge, these obscene and wrong-headed annotations are the best and most direct evidence of bad reading, and, for Coleridge, they are particularly significant because they so dramatically bring into focus that middle area between reading and criticism. The margins of the text where the reader annotates, that is, are literally the workshop in which the reading of a text becomes an understanding of that text through the use of words; analogously, these textual margins are the margins of the reader's mind where the mind confronts inscriptions and signs and makes meaning out of these signs. That Coleridge's famous annotations often contain some of his most penetrating critical insights, and often the seminal fragments of his more polished criticism, indicates, moreover, that this workshop is—at least for Coleridge—the workshop of his best literary criticism. As part of this workshop process, he suggests three distinguishable but not divisible steps (to use his own terms): reading, understanding, and an accurate and functional use of language. The matrix of the three is language; for Coleridge, not only how a reader uses language but what language he uses determines, to a great extent, the quality of his reading. More than one hundred and fifty years before the structuralists and Philippe Sollers's announcement that "the essential question today is no longer that of the *writer* and the *work* . . . but that of *writing* and *reading*," Coleridge had noted and was attempting to describe the complicated relationship between reading, language, and the critical understanding.[3]

Coleridge made it very clear that reading is itself a skill, and that varying levels of competence are the primary reason for different kinds of readers. Accordingly readers could be divided into four classes:

1. Sponges who absorb all they read, and return it nearly in the same state, only a little dirtied.

2. Sand-glasses, who retain nothing, are content to get through a book for the sake of getting through time.
3. Strain-bags, who return merely the dregs of what they read.
4. Mogul diamonds, equally rare and valuable, who profit by what they read, and enable others to profit by it also.[4]

In order to differentiate the first three categories from the serious readers, the mogul diamonds, Coleridge claims "we should . . . transfer this species of *amusement* . . . from the genus, *reading*, to that comprehensive class characterized by the power of reconciling the two contrary yet co-existing propensities of human nature, namely indulgence of sloth, and hatred of vacancy." With tongue in cheek he equates this kind of reading with "gaming, swinging, or swaying on a chair or gate; spitting over a bridge; smoking; snuff-taking; tête-à-tête after dinner between husband and wife; conning word by word all the advertisements of a daily newspaper in a public house on a rainy day, &c., &c."[5] Yet if he does dismiss a large number of readers, Coleridge also appreciates finer distinctions in reading and the quality of reading. Writing about the reception of Wordsworth's *Lyrical Ballads* he describes many readers who could have understood and enjoyed the poems on different planes, had vindictive critics not prejudiced them (*Biographia*, 1:51). And, reflecting on his own reading experience, Coleridge notices how the intelligibility of Plato alters with his own experience. He recollects "that numerous passages in this author, which I thoroughly comprehend, were formerly no less unintelligible, than the passages now in question" (1:161). In short, the comprehension and subsequent enjoyment of a text varies not only between readers but within a single reader's own lifetime.

The chief reason for these varying levels of competence

can be found in Coleridge's distinction between attending and thinking. In one of his introductory essays to *The Friend*, Coleridge demands

> THOUGHT sometimes, and ATTENTION generally. By THOUGHT I here mean the voluntary production in our minds of those states of consciousness, to which as to his fundamental facts, the Writer has referred us: while ATTENTION has for its object the order and connection of Thoughts and Images, each of which is in itself already and familiarly known. Thus the elements of Geometry require attention only; but the analysis of our primary faculties, and the investigation of all the absolute grounds of Religion and Morals, are impossible without energies of Thought in addition to the effort of Attention. . . . Both Attention and Thought are Efforts, and the latter a most difficult and laborious Effort. (*Friend*, 1:16–17)

Sponges and sand-glasses merely attend to words on a page without ever becoming actively involved in the production of meaning, while mogul diamonds and other good readers confront the text and think actively with it. Here Coleridge's position at least partially resembles Wolfgang Iser's notion of a "virtual dimension" of a text which "is not the text itself, nor is it the imagination of the reader: it is the coming together of text and imagination."[6] In this virtual dimension the reader works through the gaps and blocks that are literally and metaphorically a part of every reading experience. For both Iser and Coleridge, a text can resist, and understanding will require effort. In Coleridge's words,

> A lazy half attention amounts to a mental yawn. Where then a subject, that demands thought, has been thoughtfully treated, and with an exact and patient derivation

from its principles, we must be willing to exert a portion of the same effort, and to *think* with the author, or the author will have thought in vain for us. It makes little difference for the time being, whether there be an *hiatus oscitans* [yawning gap] in the reader's attention, or an *hiatus lacrymabilis* [lamentable gap] in the author's manuscript. (*Friend*, 1:25)

Reading should always involve the double activity of attending and thinking, an activity that Owen Barfield describes as "a polarity between understanding and understanding, a tension within the understanding itself."[7] Good reading, however, must stress the active side of this tension, where active thinking produces active understanding. In 1800, ideas supporting passive thinking and understanding, the philosophy of Hume and the psychology of David Hartley, were intellectual currency, and perhaps Coleridge's most notable contribution to modern psychology is this new emphasis on the active role of the mind in the process of understanding. To understand, especially to understand a poem, the mind must be actively engaged, and active understanding is perhaps the most crucial step on the road to criticism.

A common tendency of readers of Coleridge is to regard the understanding as a secondary and essentially negative faculty, a notion Coleridge seems to support when he remarks that this "mere *reflective* faculty partook of death" (*Biographia*, 1:144).Compared to reason, the primary moral faculty in man, understanding is indeed a derivative and secondary intelligence. But the understanding, as Barfield clarifies, plays a positive role too: "Through understanding we experience the culmination of our detachment; through imagination and the gift of reason we realize, in polarity, that very culmination as the possibility of a different and higher order of attachment."[8] In his "Theory of Life" Coleridge explains that the simultaneous experience of detachment from a material reality and of attachment to a higher reality marks the pinnacle of human consciousness, and in this context it is clear that the lifeless detachment associated with the understanding is not simply a negative state but part of a dialectical process in which understanding is an integral part. (In one sense, this is the dialectical journey that the Ancient Mariner experiences.) Ideally, understanding and reason are part of a single process in which one can distinguish the two roles without dividing them. ("It is a dull and obtuse mind that must divide in order to distinguish; but it is a still worse, that distinguishes in order to divide.")[9] "But if we are obliged to distinguish," Coleridge writes in *The Statesman's Manual*,

> we must ideally separate. In this sense . . . Reason is the knowledge of the laws of the WHOLE considered as ONE: and as such it is contradistinguished from the Understanding, which concerns itself exclusively with the quantities, qualities, and relations of *particulars* in time and space. The UNDERSTANDING, therefore, is the science of phaenomena and their subsumption under distinct kinds and sorts. . . . Its functions supply the rules and constitute the possibility of *Experience*.[10]

Reason is "the power by which we become possessed of principle" and spiritual absolutes. Understanding is "the faculty of thinking and forming *judgements*" (*Friend*, 1:177n.) and as such is the domain of reading and criticism.

Like fancy, the understanding is inherently limited in being tied to the realm of the senses. But just as fancy provides the concrete details which allow the imagination to show itself in a poem, the limitations of understanding can become a power and virtue when employed in literary criticism. Although our understanding and criticism of a poem can never embrace the total experience of that poem, this experience would remain inconsequential without the aid of the understanding. A poem reaches into the realm of reason through the power of the imagination, and a reader retrieves and communicates that experience through, first, his imagination and, second, his understanding. Coleridge writes that "Understanding and Experience may exist without Reason. But Reason cannot exist without Understanding" (*Friend*, 1:156). Here poetic vision may be substituted for reason to emphasize the role of understanding in bringing the poetic vision to life, while at the same time understanding and good criticism should always reveal themselves as the organ of reason. What is present but incommunicable in the poem "becomes, when present to the understanding, the awakener. It begins the awakening process in all men, but it can only bring it to completion when it has been discerned and, in being discerned becomes aware of itself as reason."[11] In a marginal note on Jakob Boehme, Coleridge puts this another way by distinguishing "the mode of acquiring and the mode of communicating" knowledge: the first is "Intuition, or immediate Beholding," while the second is the art of understanding "by acts of abstraction, which separate from the first are indeed mere shadows, but like shadows, of incalculable service in determining the remarkable outlines of the Substance."[12] Understanding the poem is not the experience of the poem, no more than the communicative act of good criticism is the poem. Coleridge comments on Milton's description of Death in book 3 of *Paradise Lost*: "The grandest efforts of poetry are where the imagination is called forth, not to produce a distinct form, but a strong working of the mind, still offering what is still repelled, and again creating what is again rejected; the result being what the poet wishes to impress, namely the substitution of a sublime feeling of the unimaginable for a mere image."[13] Incapable of reproducing this "sublime feeling of the unimaginable," understanding and criticism are yet informed by this vision and should serve to make the critic and the reader of the critic more conscious of it.

Coleridge probably never described this process more succinctly than in his poetic response to Wordsworth's *Prelude*, a response at once emotional, physical, and almost ineffable. The pulses of his being "beat anew," and

> Life's joy rekindling roused a throng of pain—
> Keen pangs of Love, awakening as a babe
> Turbulent, with an outcry in the heart.

His attempt to comprehend Wordsworth's poem—to understand and not simply appreciate the vision—threatens to collapse, as the experience always seems just beyond the grasp of the understanding, particularly in Coleridge's last lines:

> Scarce conscious, and yet conscious of its close
> I sate, my being blended in one thought
> (Thought was it? or aspiration? or resolve?)
> Absorbed yet hanging still upon the sound—[14]

The tension in these lines is between Coleridge's transcending intuition of *The Prelude* and what can be assimilated by his "understanding mind," the tension inherent in all criticism. Of course in writing this poem Coleridge is not writing criticism, but he is indeed reconstructing the experience out of which criticism springs—that is, the dynamics of critical response whereby the reader's understanding struggles to make what is ineffable in a poem comprehensible. The critical "understanding is in all respects a medial and mediate faculty,"[15] and here it struggles to mediate between Wordsworth's spiritual vision and the sensible forms with which Coleridge could make meaning of that vision. Wordsworth's theme is indeed "hard as high," high in its visionary reach and hard in its resistance to the tools of the understanding, specifically language: somewhat paradoxically, the poetic language of *The Prelude* contains "thoughts all too deep for words," and the dilemma of finding a *different* language to capture the nearly unspeakable experience of the poem is the principal problem both here and in all acts of critical understanding. When the language the reader-critic must substitute is discursive, moreover, the difficulties are even greater, if for no other reason than that the reader must translate from one medium to another, from poetry to prose. And in Coleridge's wide-ranging criticism, the difficulties are compounded further by the fact that there are many prose languages he might use, such as the language of science or the language of theology.

Coleridge looks once more at this problem of the role language plays in understanding a text in a long provocative note in Southey's *Life of Wesley*. This time he is writing about his own readers and readers of prose, not poetry; the emphasis, however, is still on the active participation of the reader in the construction of meaning. Years before this note, Coleridge recalls, he announced in *The Friend* that he desired "not so much to shew my Reader this or that fact, as to kindle his own touch for him, and leave it to himself to chuse the particular objects, which he might wish to examine by its light" (1:16). In *The Friend* and the *Aids to Reflection*,

the aim of every sentence is to solicit, nay *tease* the reader to ask himself, whether he *actually* does; or does not understand *distinctly?*—whether he has reflected on the precise meaning of the word, however familiar it may be both to his own ear and mouth?—whether he has been hitherto aware of the mischief and folly of employing words on questions, to know the truth of which is both his interest and his duty, without fixing

17

the one meaning which on that question they are to represent? . . . In short, I would fain bring the cause I am pleading to a short and simple, yet decisive test. Consciousness, . . . mind, life, will, body, organ—machine, nature, spirit, sin, habit, sense, understanding, reason: here are fourteen words. Have you ever reflectively and quietly asked yourself the meaning of any one of these, and tasked yourself to return the answer in *distinct* terms, not applicable to any one of the other words? Or have you contented yourself with the vague floating meaning that will just serve to save you from absurdity in the use of the word, just as the clown's botany would do, who knew that potatoes are roots, and cabbages greens? Or, if you have the gift of wit, shelter yourself under Augustine's equivocation, "I know it perfectly well till I'm asked?" Know? Ay, as an oyster knows its life. But do you know your knowledge?[16]

Coleridge's point in this passage is explicit: a text demands understanding, teases a reader for meaning, and the reader must make this meaning with language. Each word, sentence, and paragraph asks to be understood, and the reader must "return the answer in *distinct* terms." Hence, in one form, and certainly as regards reading, understanding is a product of language. According to Coleridge, all living creatures have the faculty of understanding, but only man, who possesses reason, can claim human understanding, whose proper function is "that of generalizing the notices received from the senses in order to the construction of names."[17] Animals can generalize, but, because they lack reason, cannot abstract, and without the power to abstract there can be no language:

If the power of conveying information by intelligible signs, visual or auditory, would constitute the possession of Language, Language is common to many and various animals; but if we use the word Language in its only proper sense as the power of conveying not things only but the process and result of our reflection thereon it is predicable of the Human Species alone.[18]

In his chapter on Coleridge's understanding Barfield puts this point concisely: "What renders understanding human is precisely this ability to identify by naming. . . . No abstraction, no language." The human understanding "is not only concerned with names; it is *only* concerned with names."[19] "In all instances," Coleridge claims, "it is words, names, or, if images, yet images used as words or names, that are the only and exclusive subject of understanding."[20]

The understanding of a text depends, therefore, on language to the extent that a language system is the most sophisticated way of assigning meaning. To understand a work like *The Friend* requires penetration into the exact meaning of words, which requires, in turn, finding "distinct terms" to capture that meaning. With poetic works like *The Prelude* the difficulties are even greater, since the reader is dealing with the poet's nondiscursive language, and so must attempt to translate nondiscursive meaning into a discursive language. When the reader's language is nondiscursive, in "To William Wordsworth" for instance, the strain is obvious. In each case, it is language that fashions meaning and leads the way to understanding; it is natural that Coleridge thought and wrote a good deal about the finer points of language, points which deserve some elucidation.

Though George Steiner suggests that Coleridge, along with Plato, Vico, Humboldt, Saussure, and Jakobson, is one of the few writers "who have said anything new and comprehensive" about language, surprisingly few critics have examined Coleridge's remarks on language, except to note his fascination with neologisms and precise meanings.[21] There remains much, therefore, to be done in this area, especially since the eighteenth century and first part of the nineteenth century were periods of accelerating research and writing in the philosophy of language, which interested Coleridge greatly, as did all intellectual activity. Leibniz, Hamann, Herder, Sir William Jones, Wilhelm von Humboldt, and Friedrich and August Wilhelm Schlegel all wrote extensively about the nature of language, and Coleridge was clearly stimulated by their studies. In a letter to William Godwin in 1800, Coleridge went so far as to propose a book on language,

> a book on the power of words, and the processes by which human feelings form affinities with them—in short, I wish you to philosophize Horn Tooke's System, and to solve the great Questions—whether there be reason to hold, that an action bearing all the semblance of pre-designing Consciousness may yet be simply organic, & whether a *series* of such actions are possible—and close on the heels of this question would follow the old "Is Logic the Essence of Thinking?" in other words—Is thinking impossible without arbitrary signs? &—how far is the word 'arbitrary' a misnomer?[22]

Neither Godwin nor Coleridge wrote the book, of course, but tentative and partial answers to the questions he raises here are scattered throughout his published and unpublished writings. Nearly a century before Saussure, Coleridge was attempting to break down the relation between words as signs, things, and thought, and then to reconstruct those relations into a coherent and functional philosophy of language.

Above all else, Coleridge militantly campaigns for linguistic precision:

> When two distinct meanings are confounded under one or more words, (and such must be the case, as sure as

our knowledge is progressive and of course imperfect)
erroneous consequences will be drawn, and what is true
in one sense of the word will be affirmed in toto. Men of
research, startled by the consequences, seek in the things
themselves (whether in or out of the mind) for a knowledge of the fact, and having discovered the difference,
remove the equivocations either by the substitution of a
new word, or by the appropriation of one of the two or
more words, that had before been used promiscuously.
(*Biographia*, 1:63n.)

Perhaps the foremost neologist of the nineteenth century,
Coleridge never misses an opportunity to resurrect an archaic expression or fabricate a new word in order to facilitate
clear thought. His motivations are well grounded. For Coleridge, "it is indeed never harmless to confound terms; for
words are no passive Tools, but organized Instruments, re-
acting on the Power which inspirits them."[23] With "incomparably greater ease and certainty than any other means,"
language impresses "modes of intellectual energy so constantly, so imperceptibly . . . as to secure in due time the formation of a second nature" (*Biographia*, 2:117). For this
reason, careless use of words reflects and creates dangerous
distortions of thought. "Unusual and new coined words are
doubtless an evil; but vagueness, confusion and imperfect
conveyance of our thoughts, are far greater" (1:189).

Coleridge's most famous method of refurbishing language
and guarding against murky thinking is desynonymization,
and he claims that "there are few mental exertions more
instructive, or which are capable of being rendered more
entertaining, than the attempt to establish and exemplify
the distinct meaning of terms, often confounded in common
use, and considered as mere synonyms."[24] In practice these
finer distinctions, his desynonymization of words like
agreeable, beautiful, picturesque, grand, and *sublime* are

finer, more accurate meanings; some of his most celebrated critical insights are a product of this concern with verbal precision. To use his own metaphor, Coleridge fashions his powerful saws for critical investigation by honing the razor edge of words. Thus, he finds that fancy and imagination "were two distinct and widely different faculties, instead of being according to the general belief, either two names with one meaning, or, at furthest, the lower and higher degree of one and the same power" (*Biographia*, 1:61). Similarly, the word *esemplastic* enters our vocabulary when "having to convey a new sense, I thought that a new term would both aid recollection of my meaning, and prevent its being confounded with the usual import of the word, imagination" (1:107). We could add to this list the myriad original or newly fabricated terms that Coleridge introduces into our critical lexicon: "totality of interest," "mechanical talent," "aesthetic logic," "accrescence of objectivity," "germ of character," "real-life diction," "undercurrent of feeling," "the general tissue of the style," and many others. Barfield is absolutely correct in saying "Coleridge's influence on meanings is a profounder and, in the long term, more interesting study than his additions to our stock of words,"[25] for this word-obsession is not wordplay or pedantry but a practice based on the conviction that clarity and accuracy in diction are eminently important, and that "language is happily contrived to lead us from the vague to the distinct, from the imperfect to the full and finished form."[26] The right word "becomes the point of penetration"[27] into the realm of ideas, and a manuscript note on a work of John Hunter provides a striking dramatization of this special power in words: "Still did he seem to miss the compleating Word that should have . . . reflected the Idea, . . . and have . . . placed it at the disposal of his own conscious . . . and voluntary Contemplation, . . . for the Word is the first Birth of the Idea, and its flexible Organ."[28]

This passion for an accurate correspondence between words and ideas often leads Coleridge to claim that there is a "physiognomy in words" and to speculate on destroying the "old antithesis of *Words* and *Things*, and living Things too." [29] This, however, is a dream that always dissipates in more sober moments when distance between the sign and the thing, between the sign and the idea, becomes an inescapable fact. "Coleridge's feeling for words," Barfield observes, "was an integral part of his whole deeply-felt philosophy of the true relation between words and thoughts and things, and thus, and thus only, between words and things." [30] Language does not reproduce things; it gives, rather, "outness to thought." [31] Whether we wish to designate the signified "reality" or "reason" or "idea," the signifier is at best a soft-focus symbol, and only after the idea has been revealed to the reason can there follow "communication by the symbolic use of the Understanding, which is the function of Imagination." [32]

In *Patterns of Consciousness*, Richard Haven observes that "one of Coleridge's frequently reiterated complaints concerns those who mistake the 'dead letter' for reality, who take literally what is properly figurative, who mistake 'congruous notions' for statements of absolute fact. . . . He saw words and theories composed of words as in themselves partial and inadequate." Thus Coleridge writes in a notebook entry which Haven quotes, "It is the instinct of the Letter to bring into subjection to itself the Spirit.—The latter cannot dispute—nor can it be disputed for, but with certainty of defeat. For words express generalities that can be made *so* clear—they have neither the play of colors, nor the untranslatable meanings of the eye, nor any one of the thousand undescribable things that form the whole reality of the living fuel." Haven concludes that Coleridge therefore "required of a reader that he take words not merely as signs of definitions, verbal concepts, but of symbols of what he can know only by reference to his own experience, his own 'Reason.'"[33] Besides "the language of words," Coleridge writes, "there is a language of spirits (sermo interior) and . . . the former is only the vehicle for the latter" (*Biographia*, 1:191). Thus, understanding and language stand at a considerable conceptual distance from the most significant experiences in life, and the highest truths "are reported only through the imperfect translation of lifeless and sightless *notions*. Perhaps, in a great part, through words which are but the shadows of notions; even as the notional understanding itself is but the shadowy abstraction of living and actual truth" (1:168). If on the one hand Coleridge urges precision with languages, there now seems to be a built-in deception in that precision, and Coleridge appears to contradict his own mandate when he asks "whether or no too great definiteness of Terms in any language may not consume too much of the vital & idea-creating force in distinct, clear, full made Images & so prevent originality—original thought as distinguished from positive thought."[34]

Coleridge's philosophy of language is, however, not contradictory, but only complex. These complications are what shape the role of language in his literary criticism. In the notebook entry just quoted Coleridge differentiates positive thought and original thought, and these two modes of thought correspond to the critical activity and the poetic activity, a distinction that helps explain that controversial notebook entry in which Coleridge writes, "The elder Languages [were] fitter for Poetry because they expressed only prominent ideas with clearness, others but darkly. . . . When no criticism is pretended to, & the Mind in its simplicity gives itself up to a Poem as to a work of nature, Poetry gives most pleasure when only generally & not perfectly understood."[35] That many critics quote only the last clause of this passage is what creates so much confusion and does an injustice to Coleridge's thought, for what he in fact implies is not that poetry should be imperfectly understood, but that the reading of poetry has a twofold movement: (1) "When no criticism is pretended to," the reader participates in "original thought" and in the visionary realm of ideas where, as with Coleridge's experience of *The Prelude,* thoughts are "all too deep for words"; but (2) when criticism is the object, the reader must use his understanding or "positive thought," and here language is a necessary and valuable tool. Both movements are equally important and usually operate simultaneously; moreover, the authority of language seems negligible only when one attempts to compare it with ideas and original thought. From the perspective of eternal truth, understanding and language *are* relative; each is "the faculty of suiting measures to circumstances," "of adapting means to proximate ends."[36] But as a temporal vehicle in the service of the understanding, that language is indeed authoritative and should therefore be as precise as possible, so that the understanding operates as efficiently and accurately as possible. In other words, a poem may be, as Coleridge indicates, a Kantian synolon, containing a single unique truth, but a reader can understand that truth in a variety of ways. He can write about that truth with different words and different languages, without diminishing either the nondiscursive mystery which is the center of the poem or the heuristic value of language and the understanding.

Implicitly emphasizing the relativity and variety of languages, these ideas on language and the reading experience have their roots in a philosophy which was fast becoming the most popular linguistic theory at the beginning of the nineteenth century. George Steiner outlines this trend in an article which posits two fundamental schools of linguistics, the relativists and the universalists. The universalist maintains that the underlying structure of all languages is the same and hence common to all men; the relativist holds that there are more differences than similarities in language and that those differences are the product of historical and cultural determinants. For the relativists, "no two languages construe the same world," and one of Coleridge's primary sources, Leibniz, is an early linguistic relativist who in 1697 put forward the radical proposition that language is not simply the vehicle for thought but its determining medium.[37]

From Leibniz to Coleridge, the line of relativists is quite clear, even if their philosophies of language differ on finer points. Vico, Hamann, Humboldt, and the Schlegels are the most distinguished exponents of this tradition, and Coleridge quickly assimilated and adapted their assumptions about language into his own system. In 1795 Coleridge notes that "every Age has its peculiar Language,"[38] and later in *Biographia Literaria* he elaborates: "Everyman's language varies, according to the extent of his knowledge, the activities of his faculties, and the depth or quickness of his feelings. Everyman's language has, first, its *individualities*; secondly, the common properties of the *class* to which he belongs; and thirdly, words and phrases of *universal* use" (2:41). Needless to say, it is this relativistic assumption about language which lies behind Coleridge's criticism of Wordsworth's pretense to imitate the language of the common man. "We do not adopt the language of a class," Coleridge asserts, "by the mere adoption of such words exclusively, as that class would use, at least understand; but likewise by following the *order*, in which the words of such men are wont to succeed each other" (2:43). Furthermore, as I have been indicating throughout this essay, this relativistic nature of language mirrors the relativistic role of the understanding: two people using different languages will understand a phenomenon differently. Following Leibniz, Coleridge goes so far as to suggest "language itself does as it were *think* for us" on certain occasions (1:63n).

Operating together, these three components of reading— the mediate role of the understanding in the reader's literary experience, the relative nature of language, and the functional bond between language and understanding—provide, I believe, a fresh and elucidating perspective on Coleridge's criticism and critical language. They suggest, in short, that the critical language plays a more determinant role in the reading of literature, and that those readings will be relative, in one sense, precisely because they are a product of language. That Coleridge is a relativist, especially regarding literature, will sound blasphemous in many quarters, unless one keeps in mind that we are discussing the critical understanding of a poem, not the ineffable vision of a poem—the rules for reading and judging a poem, not the principles of art. Invariably Coleridge stresses the fundamental principles of art as the foundation of criticism, but, in practice, he uses a relative language and rarely hesitates to pass judgments. The *Biographia Literaria* is perhaps the best evidence of the way Coleridge operates between these two poles, moving from principles to judgments, but like the relation between reason and understanding, the critical functions are never truly divided, just as the first part of the *Biographia* is integrally bound to the second. Critical judgments and evaluations may be the shadows of the principles from which they proceed, yet it is not "possible that the two could be separated" (2:63).

How the relativity of language actually manifests itself in Coleridge's critical writings is a more difficult point, since it would seem that the relativity of language refers to larger historical and geographical patterns which have little bearing on Coleridge's comparatively stable use of language. This stability is more apparent than real, however, and Coleridge's attitude toward contemporaneous but separate fields of knowledge sheds some light on this question. Shawcross voices what has become the common view: "It is necessary . . . to realize, first, that Coleridge did not believe in any such detached activity of the various faculties, as a physiological or psychological fact. Secondly, that although he could conceive of the mind as limiting itself, by its own free act, to a partial aspect of reality and to a partial self-activity, he saw that such an act, where it was not consciously recognized as an act of limitation, might be a fruitful source of error" (1:lxxxvi). Generally critics choose to ignore that fruitful act of limitation and examine closely the monistic vision that underlies it. But Coleridge himself recognized that if the monistic vision is the nobler, more spiritual activity, the partial kinds of knowledge in which it manifests itself are the more practical and usual way men perceive; consequently, "the man of genius devotes himself to produce by all other means, whether a statesman, a poet, a painter, a statuary, or a man of science, this same sort of something which the mind can know but which it cannot understand, of which understanding can be no more than the symbol and is only excellent as being the symbol." [39] The poet, the statesman, the scientist, that is, all have different ways of understanding because they rely on different semiotic systems, different discourses. "Reason cannot exist without Understanding; nor does it or can it manifest itself but in and through the understanding, which in our elder writers is often called *discourse*, or discursive faculty . . . and an understanding enlightened by reason Shakespear[e] gives as the contradistinguishing character of man, under the name of *discourse of reason*" (*Friend*, 1:156).

In Coleridge's time it was possible to isolate a number of different discourses, such as a scientific discourse, psychological discourse, or theological discourse, all of which have their own means of organizing signs for the attribution of meaning, as well as special connotations which carry over when these languages transfer to other disciplines. Clearly the distances between the separate discourses were not as great as they would become in the twentieth century, when Steiner would point out that mathematics, music, psychology, and other disciplines have each developed a specialized language which is nearly incomprehensible to an outsider. But the differences between the languages of contemporary fields of knowledge were great enough in 1816 for Coleridge to discern an "Alphabet of Physics no less than of Metaphysics, of Physiology no less than of Psychology."[40] Each of these discourses would be working toward the same truth, would eventually apprehend the same reality, but the mode of understanding would be significantly different and certainly relative. Coleridge asks "why facts were ever called stubborn things? . . . Facts, you know are not truths."[41] Thus a poet and a scientist could describe the same reality in different ways; they could present different facts which follow from an identical truth. More important, when the literary critic employs a scientific discourse, literature will necessarily be understood in an idiosyncratic way and special "facts" will appear in that criticism. Describing poetry with scientific terms, as Coleridge does in the *Biographia Literaria*, is not an innocent act.

What creates these separate discourses is primarily their audiences. Recent linguists argue convincingly that languages and their laws are determined by a "circuit of discourse," so that what is understood between speaker and hearer delineates the perimeters of that language. For Coleridge also, the readers or listeners predetermine the kind of discourse an author chooses. "Be the work good or evil in its tendency, in both cases alike there is one question to be predetermined, viz. what class or classes of the reading world the work is intended for."[42] Readers

are not seldom picked and chosen. . . . If the Author have clearly and rightly established in his own mind the class of readers, to which he means to address his communications; and if both in this choice, and in the particulars of the manner and matter of the work, he

conscientiously observes all the conditions which reason and conscience have been shewn to dictate, in relation to those for whom the work was designed; he will,
in most instances, have effected his design and realized
the desired circumscription. The posthumous work of
Spinoza . . . may, indeed, accidentally fall into the hands
of an incompetent reader. But (not to mention that it is
written in a dead language) it will be entirely harmless, because it needs be utterly unintelligible. (*Friend*,
1:53–54)

Pedantry "consists in the use of words unsuitable to the
time, place, and company. The language of the market would
be in the schools as pedantic, . . . as the languages of the
schools in the market. The mere man of the world, who insists that no other terms but such as occur in common conversation would be employed in a scientific disquisition, and
with no greater precision, is as truly a pedant as the man
of letters, who either overrating the acquirements of his au-
ditors, or misled by his own familiarity with technical or
scholastic terms, converses at the wine table with his mind
fixed on his museum or laboratory" (*Biographia*, 1:107–8).
Therefore, to avoid pedantry and to be understood, a writer
must carefully choose his audience and his occasion; he
must choose a specific discourse. If we recall the mutual dependence of understanding and language, moreover, these
choices become a major determinant in how and what a
critic understands when he reads. "In reading," Philipe Sollers says, "we must become aware of what we write unconsciously in our reading,"[43] an insight which corroborates
Coleridge's note on Boehme, where Coleridge equates understanding with the "mode of communicating." How literary critics understand a poem and what they understand
about it follow from the audience they foresee and the language they adapt. Sometimes—mostly in the twentieth cen-

tury—this audience and language is exclusively literary, to the point of being rarified. With Coleridge this is rarely the case. His critical language is usually a mixture of scientific, psychological, and theological discourses, one or another being dominant depending on when and for whom he is writing.

The important point, then, is that language is a singularly exact tool in literary criticism, suited for specific purposes and specific audiences, suited to enable a person to understand in a certain way. For Coleridge, some of the ways of understanding would be scientific, political, theological, or philosophical. Indeed these may be simply distinctions not divisions; "nevertheless, it is of great practical importance, that these distinctions should be made and understood" (*Friend*, 1:177), especially regarding their effect on Coleridge's literary criticism. For different ways of reading, different kinds of criticism, and different meanings very often amount to approaching and understanding a text with different languages. In his criticism Coleridge translates his poetic experiences into discursive, extraliterary languages, and these translations do not just rephrase meaning: in many ways they make meaning. Many critics overlook this last point, but M. H. Abrams realized it many years ago in *The Mirror and the Lamp*, when he discussed the role of metaphor in literary criticism:

> The task of analyzing the nature and function of metaphor has traditionally been assigned to the rhetorician and to the critic of literature. Metaphor, however, whether alive or moribund, is an inseparable element of all discourse, including discourse whose purpose is neither persuasive nor aesthetic, but descriptive and informative. . . . And in the criticism of poetry, metaphor and analogy, though less conspicuous, are hardly less than in poetry itself. . . . While many expository analogues . . .

are causal and illustrative, some few seem recurrent and, not illustrative, but constructive: they yield the ground plan and essential structural elements of a literary theory. . . . By the same token, they select and mold these "facts" which a theory comprehends. For facts are *facta*, things made as much as things found, and made in part by the analogies through which we look at the world as through a lens.[44]

Just as the understanding can produce diverse facts from a single truth, so extraliterary discourse can produce different readings of one poem by translating that poem into a cultural language outside the poem.

Translation is in fact not an adventitious term with which to describe this process, for the art of translation is an elucidating analogue for the critical process. Coleridge himself employs the term freely and would certainly have concurred with Steiner's far-reaching definition:

Translation, properly understood, is a special case of the arc of communication which every successful speech act closes with a given language. On the inter-lingual level, translation will pose concentrated, visibly intractable problems; but these same problems abound, at a more covert or conventionally neglected level, intralingually. The model "sender to receiver" which represents any semiological and semantic process is ontologically equivalent to the model "source-language to receptor-language" used in the theory of translation. In both schemes there is "in the middle" an operation of interpretive decipherment, an encoding-decoding function of synapse.[45]

A poet encodes a complex statement of feeling and thought by means of a poetic idiom. Unless the critic wishes to follow Borges's Pierre Menard and simply rewrite the original text, he must decode and recode the text into a different language, which, for Coleridge, is one and the same process: understanding-with-language. Especially in poetry the translation which criticism entails can only approximate the original and involves the sacrifice of finer shades of meaning. "In poetry," Coleridge writes,

> in which every line, every phrase, may pass the ordeal of deliberation and deliberate choice, it is possible . . . to attain the ultimatum which I have ventured to propose as the infallible test of a blameless style; its *untranslatableness* in words of the same language without injury to the meaning. Be it observed, however, that I include in the *meaning* of a word not only its correspondent object, but likewise all the associations which it recalls. For language is framed to convey not the object alone, but likewise the character, mood, and intentions of the person who is representing it. (*Biographia*, 2:115–16)

This untranslatable meaning is surely part of the problem we witness in "To William Wordsworth," and probably accounts for the anxiety that underlies Coleridge's notes to "Religious Musings," in which he literally translates his lines of poetry into scriptural passages or the psychological lexicon of David Hartley.

The process of translation involved in criticism is not, however, necessarily a destructive practice and the anxiety of criticism is usually exaggerated. In "On Linguistic Aspects of Translation," Roman Jakobson, like Coleridge, sees poetry as untranslatable and suggests that explication will never comprehend the full force of a poem. But "creative transposition" is possible from one set of signs to another, from one code to another: "either intralingual transposition—from one poetic shape to another, or interlingual transposition—from one language into another."[46] By inter-semiotic transposition Jakobson means translating from literature to cinema, for example. But, given the fundamental semantic differences between poetry and extraliterary prose, creative transposition is equally possible in criticism: the good critic, through the particular language he uses, can and should actualize the meaning of a text in an interesting and significant manner, thus compensating for the anxiety of omission.

I am most definitely not attempting to masquerade Coleridge as a structuralist; I am attempting to show that there is a structuralist attitude with which Coleridge would have been sympathetic and which, applied to Coleridge's critical writings, elucidates them. While literature would surround Coleridge throughout his career, nonliterary disciplines would become the temporary center of his work at differing times and for differing reasons. Invariably the challenge of these other fields permeates his literary criticism and demands poetic meaning to be made in their terms, often as an entirely conscious process and sometimes as an unconscious act in which reading and writing merge. During his early years of political fervor, political rhetoric clearly controls his scattered comments on art and literature; in 1815 Coleridge's involvement in the medical controversy over the writings of John Hunter not only results in his scientific treatise "Theory of Life" but leads Coleridge to write *Biographia Literaria* with a scientific language that would influence literary criticism for well over a century. In his last years Coleridge would deliver one of the most puzzling lectures on Aeschylus's *Prometheus* ever written, a lecture that can be explained only by Coleridge's immersion in the theological discourse found in his essays *On the Constitution of the Church and State*. In each of these cases, Coleridge translates his poetic experiences into discursive, extraliterary languages which do not just rephrase meaning but in many ways make meaning. Without diminishing the specific truth at the heart of a particular poem, Coleridge uses an extraliterary language to actualize that truth, to make its meaning speak to a certain audience, to extend poetry's significance obtrusively beyond the realm of literature. With his acute sensitivity to language and its powers, Coleridge becomes a Protean reader, a chameleon critic, who uses different languages as subtle but powerful interpretive systems to determine what literature means, for whom. Certainly a penetrating and incisive reader, Coleridge is likewise an expansive reader. For him, the margins both of the text and of the mind are always wide.

CHAPTER TWO

The Politics of Rhetoric in Coleridge's Early Criticism

*Talk not with scorn of Authors—it was the
chattering of the Geese that saved the Capitol.*
COLERIDGE, 1802

DURING THE ROMANTIC PERIOD the political and social conscience which informs so much of eighteenth-century literary criticism is generally believed to have lost its distinctly pragmatic edge. For many, consequently, Shelley's ethereal *Defense of Poetry* is a prototypically Romantic document whose visionary poetics represent a common tendency among Romantics to avoid the hurly-burly of social and political facts. The education and salvation of society remains of course a pressing concern for the vast majority of Romantic writers, and Shelley's classic essay does conclude with the breathless claim that "poets are the unacknowledged legislators of the world." But the immediate and concrete realities of parliamentary legislators and quotidian politics that permeate the writings of Samuel Johnson in the eighteenth century and the work of Georg Lukács and the young Auden in the twentieth are indeed mostly ignored in Romantic literary criticism. However politically aware and socially involved Shelley and Wordsworth may have been as individuals, they usually keep the specifics of politics out of their writings on literature. Moreover, when connections between poetry and politics are made by these writers, it is usually the eternal truths of poetry that determine their judgments on daily politics: words like *liberty* may appear in their poetics, but not the names of Jamaican slave-traders.

Coleridge's early writings on literature, however, are a notable and overlooked exception to this practice, since in the 1790s Coleridge reverses the methods of his ethereal contemporaries by allowing political opinions and political exigencies often to determine not only what poetry he reads but what he finds there. Writing to T. B. Street later in his life he asks, "For who in the Devil's Name ever thought of reading Poetry for any political or practical purposes till these Devil's Times that *we* live in?"[1] In the context of the letter, this statement is clearly less praise than abuse of a kind of criticism in which political questions influence literary tastes. Yet, years earlier, Coleridge enthusiastically practiced this kind of criticism in his notebooks, marginalia, and periodical reviews. The 1790s are in many respects Coleridge's most political years, and these are accordingly the years of his most obtrusive political literary criticism, the years in which daily politics and the language of politics play not only an important but a constitutive role in his critical judgments. Perhaps literary criticism's most renowned idealist, in these early years Coleridge practices a literary criticism as firmly rooted in the sweat and mire of daily events as the work of our best Marxist critics, a literary criticism defined by a politics of language as well as the language of politics.

In the 1790s current events were naturally the consuming passion of all intellectuals like Coleridge. The French Revolution released energies that had been building throughout Europe, and in England it triggered a chain of events that became the center of Coleridge's life and work until the turn of the century. The events and individuals that most directly affected Coleridge are well documented by Coleridge scholars,[2] and Coleridge himself has left a fairly thorough account of his reaction to the times in his lectures of 1795 and his essays for the *Morning Post* and the *Courier*. England's war with France, Napoleon, the Treason and Sedition Bills of 1795, and Pitt were the main issues for Coleridge, yet these necessarily involved him in more specific problems like the debate over the abolition of slavery, Lord Grenville, the challenge of commerce and industry, the state trials of Tooke, Hardy, and Thelwall, as well as the writings of Godwin and Paley. Years later, Coleridge would insist that admidst all this political disturbance he positioned himself "almost equidistant from all three prominent parties, the Pittites, the Foxites, and the Democrats."[3] But although there is some truth in this recollection, most scholars have rightly doubted its complete accuracy. (Coleridge's rather selective editing of some of his youthful lectures for *The Friend* is reason enough for skepticism.) If in his own mind Coleridge maintains a cool and distant perspective on events after the French Revolution, he nevertheless combats the Tory government with a rhetoric as heated as any Jacobin's. Indeed, he eventually renounces the radicalism of his youth, and, like Wordsworth, in his later years embraces more conservative views with as much conviction as he had his early politics. In Alfred Cobban's words, "Coleridge, who had escaped the panic when all around were scenting treason and Jacobinism in every corner, with a contrariety which might have been insight, began, as soon as the anti-Jacobin cry had died down to discover some need for it, and by the time of the after-war distresses was in a very fever of apprehension."[4] The reason for this change, however, is not so much Coleridge's capricious mind, but rather the change in England's political climate—at least as Coleridge saw it. For when Pitts's tyrannical Tory government wielded power, the radical rhetoric of men like Coleridge was a corrective measure; as the uneducated middle class gained more and more political power after 1800, this same Jacobin rhetoric would be extremely dangerous, because it would be in the hands of the mostly ignorant masses. Add to this France's invasion of Switzerland in 1798 and her treacherous treatment of Spain, and Coleridge's politics seem not only logical but consistent.

Yet if Coleridge's politics became more sober, he could

never completely extricate himself from them, no matter how much he protests or what he tries to substitute for them. As early as 1796, he claims that "local and temporary Politics are my aversion—they narrow the understanding, they narrow the heart, they fret the temper."[5] The facts, however, contradict him. Coleridge could probably not make Wordsworth's hyperbolic claim about giving "twelve hours thought to the condition and prospect of society for one to poetry." Still, especially in these early years, Coleridge regularly and sometimes fiercely struggles to reconcile politics and political questions with his other beliefs and pursuits. His prose works of this period are the best testimonies in this regard: *The Watchman* and the *Lectures 1795 on Politics and Religion* directly confront most of the major political topics of the day, and invariably attempt to relate them to larger cultural concerns. To be sure, religion is one of these concerns, and in his last years I believe theology ultimately dominates politics to the extent that his political judgments follow from certain theological ideas. In the 1790s the reverse is true, so that his 1795 *Lectures on Revealed Religion* often read like political tracts in which Christ's most significant teachings concern social democracy. In his introduction to these lectures Peter Mann observes: "That Christ was a 'reformer' was a common theme in the reform literature of the 1790s, but Coleridge was alone in drawing upon the latent political philosophy in the New Testament and in the Old in so extreme a way."[6] Doubtless his religion would influence his politics in some important ways during these years and it accounts for his complex and critical feelings about Godwin, Holcraft, and Thelwall, good revolutionaries who were unfortunately infidels. And given the salient moral dimension of his politics during this time, his politics are frequently better described as a morality, though a morality with a distinctly pragmatic coloring that differentiates it from the morality of the 1820s. If Coleridge is obsessed with politics at this time, they are the politics about which Rousseau says in the last book of *Emile*: "Those who want to treat morality and politics separately will never understand anything about either." When put into practice, moreover, this inclusion of ethics or moral psychology within the terms of politics naturally becomes a crucial dimension of his language at this time.

Besides religion and morality, another extremely important pursuit that comes under the umbrella of Coleridge's politics is of course literature and the poetry he is writing at this time. Above all a man of letters, Coleridge never becomes so deeply involved in his politics that he can forget his first calling, poetry. Literature's role and his own poetry's role in particular in these times of crisis would hence have been of crucial concern to him. As Coleridge quickly discovered, in all periods of social crisis the realm of the imagination is pressured to justify itself: whatever one's political position, social action becomes equated with meaning, and if literature wishes to have meaning it must defend itself as a form of social action. Coleridge's "Reflections on Having Left a Place of Retirement" is a personal version of this problem. Written in 1795 when Coleridge was enjoying the poetic solitude of a "quiet Dell! . . . and Mount sublime!" it asks the question,

> Was it right
> While unnumber'd brethren toil'd and bled,
> That I should dream away the entrusted hours
> On rose-leaf beds, pampering the coward heart
> With feelings all too delicate for use?

Coleridge's rhetorical answer is no, that these socially critical times demand a socially active response. He must therefore leave his dreamy poetic world and

go, and join head, heart, and hand,
Active and firm, to fight the bloodless fight
Of Science, Freedom, and the Truth in Christ.[7]

Yet, as Coleridge himself soon realizes, he would look silly on the barricades, and his political involvement would have to be more oblique than John Thelwall's. His would have to be a "bloodless fight." "I am not *fit* for *public* Life," he writes Thelwall, "yet the Light shall stream to a far distance from the taper in my cottage window."[8] Clearly this is not an admission of defeat, just a clarification of means. In 1795 Coleridge says, "It should be infamous for a Man, who has reached the years of discretion, not to have formed an opinion concerning the state of affairs in his country, and treasonable, having formed one, not to propagate it by every legal means in his power" (*Lectures 1795*, p. 54). For Coleridge, the means would be oral and written language, essays, and lectures, not street fighting. Moreover, poetry and politics, he found, do not preclude each other. Poetry can be political, and Coleridge's departure from the bucolic world does not mean he must forsake poetry, but perhaps only a kind of poetry. Carl Woodring's book on the politics in Coleridge's poetry is the most thorough demonstration of the extent to which Coleridge's poetry becomes at this time the vehicle for his politics. Even a casual glance at Coleridge's poetry of this period shows how decidedly contemporary politics and the language of politics served to actuate his imaginative work. From his juvenile "Destruction of the Bastille" to the "Sonnets on Eminent Characters" and "Religious Musings," political events and characters are the vehicle, and political feeling the tenor, of the majority of his poems.[9]

The way to actuate poetry politically is not, however, limited to the writing of political poems; there is a way to read and criticize which also actuates literature, his own as well as others. Significantly, Coleridge himself coined the word *actualize*, for he, perhaps more than any critic of his day, practices a kind of criticism that attempts to actuate literature by merging the language of literature with the language of politics. For Coleridge, the principles behind all good poems are the same that motivate morally sound politics. Poetry and art therefore have political implications, since they communicate the same principles that should resound through the world of politics in all times. Thus, *Paradise Lost* is as politically relevant to England in the 1790s as Coleridge's own "Religious Musings." Unfortunately the political relevance of nontopical works of literature like *Paradise Lost* is so invariably ignored by his contemporary readers and critics that their political impact is neutralized. Moreover, neutralized, the poetry that should motivate the reader to political action becomes, with tragic irony, an escape from the brutal facts of contemporary life. The outrage of this kind of literary sensibility which is so socially unfeeling leads Coleridge to observe in his notebook: "Poetry—excites us to artificial feelings—makes us callous to real ones."[10] And in *The Watchman* he distinguishes the politically loaded word *benevolence* from the aristocratic *sensibility* in a barbed tirade against apolitical citizens and apolitical readers of Goethe and Richardson:

> There is observable among the Many a false and bastard sensibility that prompts them to remove those evils and those evils alone, which by hideous spectacle or clamorous outcry are present to their senses, and disturb their selfish enjoyments. Other miseries, though equally certain and far more horrible, they not only do not endeavor to remedy—they support, they fatten on them. Provided the dunghill be not before the parlor window, they are well content to know that it exists, and that it is the hot bed of their pestilent luxuries. To this griev-

45

ous failing we must attribute the frequency of wars, and
the continuance of the Slave-trade. The merchant finds
no argument against it in his ledger. . . . The fine lady's
nerves are not shattered by the shrieks! She sips a bev-
erage sweetened with human blood, even while she is
weeping over the refined sorrows of Werter or of Clem-
entina. Sensibility is not Benevolence. Nay, by making
us trembling alive to trifling misfortunes, it frequently
prevents it, and induces effeminate and cowardly selfishness. . . . Benevolence impels to action.[11]

Directly opposed to this kind of reader, in the 1790s Coleridge reads and criticizes literature with a political consciousness that is not only topical but often quite tenden-
tious. More specifically, when Coleridge reads literature,
political terms and favorite political figures frequently become part of his critical judgments and serve as interpretive
standards which give contemporary political meaning to the
realm of art and imagination. For Coleridge, in short, politics
and literature coincide, and the reader should make that coincidence unmistakably apparent so that the flesh-and-blood
significance of poetry is not lost.

Even more to the point are some of Coleridge's textual
notes to "Religious Musings." As if he worried that the political meaning of this already very political poem would be
missed by aristocratic aesthetes, he himself interprets lines
for the reader, thus providing his own political commentary
on the text. At one point the poetry reads:

But first offences need must come! Even now
(Black Hell laughs horrible—to hear the scoff!)
Thee to defend, meek Galilaean!

Coleridge's note then glosses this passage with a long account of the Earl of Guilford's and the Duke of Bedford's

46

parliamentary motions for peace with France in 1794, and the Duke of Portland's and Lord Abingdon's successful defense of the war as a Christian cause. In another passage, Coleridge exclaims rather explicitly:

> From all sides rush the thirsty brood of War!—
> Austria, and that foul Woman of the North,
> The lustful murdress of her wedded lord!
> And he, connatural Mind!

But, lest some reader mistake this last reference to Frederick William II, King of Prussia, for a poetic trope, Coleridge explains: "That Despot who received the wages of an hireling that he might act the part of a swindler, and who skulked from his impotent attacks on the liberties of France to perpetrate more successful iniquity in the plains of *Poland*."[12] In each of these instances, Coleridge's critical commentary and notes are intended to give the poetry political meaning and to bring it into the realm of social action.[13] Although politics and the language of politics may not have a prior claim on poetry, they do accentuate and elucidate a frequently ignored dimension of poetry, a dimension that is in every sense vital. These commentaries are thus rather explicit examples of the way Coleridge's critical language vitalizes a text through the referential and connotative force of a specifically political terminology.

Coleridge clearly recognized and even became preoccupied with this constitutive power in language and its political implications in the 1790s, for political rhetoric was proving itself in action with frightening effectiveness. Many years later, he would remark about Horne Tooke: "It shows a base and unpoetical mind to convert so beautiful, so divine, a subject as language into the vehicle or make-weight of political squibs."[14] However, at this time, Coleridge had little control over how language was used and his social conscience forced him to join political debates that often focused on language. In the 1790s language was nothing if not political, and Coleridge's duty was to see that language at least served the right politics. "In attacking the Pitt Ministry," John Colmer explains in *Coleridge: Critic of Society*, "Coleridge was led to reflect on one problem that was to engage his attention throughout his life, the principles that should regulate the use of the spoken or written word to influence public opinion on controversial issues. His preoccupation with the rights and duties involved in any attempt to communicate moral and political truth was the natural outcome of his recognition of the power of the written and spoken word."[15]

Coleridge's most cogent statements on the power of language and its abuse are two political articles written for the *Morning Post* in 1800, one entitled "Lord Grenville's Note" and the other being a Plutarchian sketch of Pitt. The first begins with a passage that is central to any understanding of Coleridge and his philosophy of language: "We think *in* words, and reason *by* words.—The man who, while he is speaking or writing his native language, uses words inaccurately, and combines them inconsequently, may be fairly presumed to be a lax and slovenly reasoner." The consequences of this lax reasoning and slovenly language are indeed great, especially in the 1790s: "False reasoning is perhaps never wholly harmless; but it becomes an enormous evil, when the reasoning, and the passions which accompany it, are to be followed by the sacrifice of tens of thousands."[16] The chief perpetrator of treacherous language is Pitt, whose "mind was founded and elemented in words and generalities" but "whose heart was solitary" and thus lacked sensibility and morality. Pitt may be a wizard with language, but, because he is without moral feeling, his language becomes an instrument of evil. An "inconceivably large portion of human knowledge and human power is involved in the science and management of words," and because of this power, language is especially dangerous in the service of someone as shallow as Pitt and his lackeys. Coleridge accuses Pitt of intentionally misusing words and employing vapid "generalities—Atheism and Jacobinism—phrases, which he learnt from Mr. Burke, but without learning the philosophical definitions and involved consequences, with which that man accompanied those words."[17] In "The Plot Discovered" Coleridge observes that "our minister's meaning generally bears an inverse proportion to the multitude of his words," and he claims that the new Sedition Bills are, in fact, a conspiracy of language: "The old Treason Laws are superseded by the exploded commentaries of obsequious Crown lawyers, the commentary has conspired against the text" (*Lectures 1795*, p. 296, 288).

Coleridge battles Pitt and his language on every front, redefining terms and carefully dissecting Tory rhetoric. In many cases this means inventing new words for the language of politics, just as he fabricates new words for the language of literary criticism. Except for *clerisy* most of these neologisms have faded from our vocabulary. But, as Colmer points out, "His semantic sense served him well in other ways in his political writings; it helped on many occasions to demonstrate the paucity of his opponent's arguments and to show that many questions were fundamentally questions of terminology and logomachy."[18] Thus, the center of many of Coleridge's arguments is very often simply the redefining of a key term like *benevolence, egotism,* or *patriotism,* which his opponents have distorted to serve their own purposes. His first Bristol lecture, for example, consists fundamentally of four definitions of four types of patriot, from the "dough-baked Patriots" who lack firm principles to "thinking and disinterested Patriots" (*Lectures 1795*, pp. 8, 12). To be sure, many of these terms which are central to Coleridge's literary criticism and political essays at this time may, as

I have indicated, suggest moral, religious, or even psychological meanings. But in the social context of the period—from which this language derives its overriding connotative force—these other shadings become clearly and intentionally subservient to the political and social significance that Coleridge and other writers demanded from them.

The main arenas for this fight with words were journals and reviews, the more conservative of which Coleridge called "a kind of establishment" (Notebooks, vol. 1, no. 131). In The Watchman Coleridge quotes Thomas Beddoes's opinion of these journals, which were all the more dangerous because of their party affiliation and the power of political rhetoric: "All that is required is to lie boldly, not skillfully; and four journalists will do more towards maddening the people than four hundred prudent persons, privately uttering their honest sentiments towards keeping them within the bounds of reason" (p. 309). Naturally the literary criticism that appeared in these journals makes little pretense of keeping politics out of art. Literature too becomes a sounding board for politics in every major journal and newspaper in England, and writing to Southey in 1795 Coleridge sarcastically remarks "that Albion's Longinii (the British Critics, I mean) have manifested their unshaken Zeal for political & religious orthodoxy without any weak scrupulosity about the means." [19] Later, from a pinnacle of uninvolvement, Coleridge would rail against unprincipled reviewers of any party. However, in the 1790s I believe Coleridge's vehement dislike of reviewers arose less from their criticizing literature with a political slant and political language than from the party they chose to support. The fact is that Coleridge himself uses politics and political language in his literary judgments. And, though it is unlikely he would concede this point, his only real argument is not with political criticism in journals but with the politics of the criticism. It is not political language that tarnishes literary criticism but the politics of the language.

Unlike the explicit political explanations that are attached to "Religious Musings," Coleridge's views usually enter his interpretations of literature in an unobtrusive and subtle manner, often depending on the connotations of a single word like *egotism* or *benevolence* or semantic clusters surrounding that word. Anyone familiar with Coleridge's essay "Lord Grenville's Note" will not be surprised at this quiet though effective interpretive power in Coleridge's language, for in this essay he performs nearly a word-by-word analysis of Grenville's proclamation and demonstrates how single words can control and distort meaning in any piece of writing. In a similar manner, Coleridge does not hesitate to use his own political language when he reads and criticizes poetry, thus shaping and controlling the meaning of the primary text with the critical terms he chooses or with the digressions that surround particular points.

Since a critic's language will always direct him to certain features of the primary text, this political language in Coleridge's literary criticism necessarily leads him to focus on special details and processes in literature. Almost exclusively, then, Coleridge's comments on literature at this time highlight the personality behind the work of art, a literary character, or the audience of that work. It is crucial to note, though, that his pronouncements on the artist or the audience at this point in his career differ significantly from his later psychological criticism of the expressive and affective subtleties in poetry. Praising a poem for the writer's "benevolence" is clearly different from the more complicated, teutonic criticism of Shakespeare's mind. The difference is the difference of two languages, one political, the other psychological. Indeed, Hartley is the specter in both Coleridge's political and psychological work. But Hartley's writings influence Coleridge's literary criticism in strikingly different ways, depending on Coleridge's predominant interest at the time. During Coleridge's political days, Hartley helps him fashion key terms like *benevolence* and *egotism*, which Coleridge exploits for their political significance and which he then applies to literature, while years later in the lectures on Shakespeare, Coleridge's discussion of the imagination and its literary significance swerves from Hartley toward German psychology and metaphysics.

Frequently then, Coleridge uses a poem merely as a window into the poet's heart, where Coleridge finds either a good, ethical writer who will be a good, sensitive citizen or a hard-hearted egotist who will insidiously undermine society. In a notebook, for instance, Coleridge quotes from Ben Jonson's preface to *Volpone* to the effect that a good poet must be simply a good man, the word *good* implying the social benevolence that distinguishes Coleridge's political heroes: "If men will impartially and not a'squint look toward the offices and function of a Poet, they will easily conclude to themselves the impossibility of any man's being the good Poet without being first a good man" (*Notebooks*, vol. i, no. 1057). For Coleridge, Milton is the paradigm for the good poet, and he and his work certainly seem to validate Coleridge's sociopolitical literary criticism. Colmer points out that "for Coleridge and others Milton had become a symbolic figure to represent the double opposition against the party of Church and King. It may have been the example of Milton, who gave up the middle years of his life to political controversy, as much as the influence of the radical agitators whom he met in London, that led him to abandon for the time being all thoughts of ideal systems of government and to enter the political life of his own country."[20] Moreover, the social responsibility and virtue of Milton, the man, was matched by the greatness and virtue of Milton, the poet: the same language could describe both the politician and the artist, and thus confirm the commensurability of the two worlds.

There are in this regard two particular words, *egotism* and *benevolence*, that become the most important terms for Coleridge when he distinguishes a good poem from a bad poem, a good poet from a bad poet; when he describes, that is, the heart of a poem, which for him is the heart of the poet. The first of these, *egotism*, is particularly slippery, on the one hand implying the pride and selfishness of Pitt and later of Napoleon, and on the other suggesting the confidence and bravery of a Milton. The best known instance of Coleridge's use of this term to analyze literature is his interpretation of Milton's Satan, a passage which deserves to be quoted in full, because its language so explicitly relates contemporary politics, egotism, and literature:

> The character of Satan is pride and sensual indulgence, finding in self the sole motive for action. It is the character so often seen *in little* on the political stage. It exhibits all the restlessness, temerity, and cunning which have marked the mighty hunters of mankind from Nimrod to Napoleon. The common fascination of men is, that these great men, as they are called must act from some great motive. Milton has carefully marked in his Satan the intense selfishness, the alcohol of egotism, which would rather reign in hell than serve in heaven. To place this lust of self in opposition to denial of self or duty, and to show what exertions it would make, and what pains endure to accomplish its end, is Milton's particular object in the character of Satan.[21]

Commenting on this passage, Benjamin T. Sankey argues that it derives from two primary concerns, the second of which is "the political problem of interpreting Bonaparte and his relationship to the ideals of the French Revolution."[22]

However, given the language of the passage, the concrete rhetoric of "restlessness, temerity, and cunning," this second issue seems to me to be far more important to this interpretation than the philosophical and psychological questions that Sankey points out also underlie it. Coleridge had thought and written a good deal about Napoleon by this time: his character had become nearly an archetypal model of an evil that had grave moral and political consequences. And for Coleridge this model and language, this total selfishness that knows no conflict, was consequently suited not only for the current political scourge of Europe but likewise for the first of the political blackguards, Satan.

The charge of egotism, though, is not necessarily a negative criticism of an author or character, since a word such as this, which at another time might have a single psychological meaning, has at this time a shifting significance ultimately dependent on its sociopolitical import. Coleridge may object to a sensual brand of egotism like Napoleon's, but men like Milton, Robespierre, and even John Thelwall are egotistical in an admirably patriotic way. In an early political lecture, Coleridge explains that there is a virtuous and courageous egotism different from the "disgusting Egotisms of an affected Humility" (*Lectures 1795*, p. 15). And, in his preface to the first edition of his *Poems on Various Subjects*, he remarks on the common misunderstanding of egotism, while concomitantly introducing the term into his lexicon of literary criticism:

> There is one species of Egotism which is truly disgusting; not that which leads us to communicate our feelings to others, but that which would reduce the feelings of others to an identity with our own. The Atheist, who exclaims, "pshaw!" when he glances his eye on the praises of Deity, is an Egotist: an old man, when he speaks contemptuously of Love-verses, is an Egotist: and

the sleek favourites of fortune are Egotists, when they condemn all "melancholy, discontented" verses. . . . Men old and hackneyed in the ways of the world are scrupulous avoiders of egotism.[23]

"Compositions, resembling those of the present volume," he writes, "are not unfrequently condemned for their querulous Egotism. But egotism is to be condemned then only when it offends against time and place, as in a history or an epic poem. To censure it in a monody or sonnet is almost as absurd as to dislike a circle for being round." Further, he bitingly observes the hypocritical fashion of contemporary writers: "With what anxiety every fashionable author avoids the word *I!*—now he transforms himself into a third person; 'the present writer' now multiplies himself and swells into 'we'; and all this is the watchfulness of guilt. Conscious that this said *I* is perpetually intruding on his mind and that it monopolizes his heart, he is prudishly solicitous that it may not escape from his lips."[24] Hence, Goldsmith's "Deserted Village" and Abraham Cowley's verse essay on Cromwell are disparaged because they are "without the passion, or the peculiar feeling" of a healthy egotism (*Notebooks*, vol. 1, no. 829), and Southey's sonnets are praised for their "manly yet gentle Egotism."[25]

Continuing to transpose this term, so clearly related to social individualism and a kind of political heroism, into a standard for literary judgments, Coleridge claims that "poetry without egotism" is "comparatively uninteresting" (*Notebooks*, vol. 1, no. 62). And, finding "no title more descriptive of the manner and matter of the poems," he describes his first poems as "effusions," a word that suggests the healthy egotism needed for good poetry and good politics and, more important, echoes the political language of a 1795 poetry review in *The British Critic*. The review, part of which Coleridge transcribes in his notebook, extols the Rev.

William Hett's "humble endeavors" as "Effusions . . . of real patriotism and attachment to our existing Constitution."[26] Borrowing the word, Coleridge uses it as an interpretive title and consequently associates his poems with an egotism that is "real patriotism," thus giving even his apolitical poems political significance. (Aptly, he changed the title later, when his political ardor cooled.)

Coleridge's second preface to the same volume of poems answers a criticism related to this same term, *egotism*—a criticism that is political as well as linguistic and that generates another standard for literary evaluations through the opposition that Coleridge establishes between political and poetic obscurity. After pleading guilty to the "profusion of double-epithets, and a general turgidness," he attempts to acquit himself of a greater fault: "A third and heavier accusation has been brought against me, that of obscurity; but not, I think, with equal justice. An Author is obscure when his conceptions are dim and imperfect, and his language incorrect, or inappropriate, or involved. A poem that abounds in allusions, like the Bard of Gray, or one that impersonates high and abstract truths, like Colin's Ode on the Poetical Character, claims not to be popular—but should be acquited of obscurity."[27] Obscurity could be a harsh criticism, one that Coleridge himself had leveled against political speakers many times. It is an abuse of language, practiced in Parliament often with tragic results, and an abuse he discusses at length in *The Watchman* (p. 55). Yet the kind of obscurity that Coleridge defends here as poetically valuable must be distinguished from legislative obscurity, for in poems obscurity can be an artistic strategy. Later that year, Coleridge makes these comments on Milton's sometimes obscure poetry: "A Reader of Milton must be always on his Duty: he is surrounded with sense; it rises in every line; every word is to the purpose. There are no lazy intervals: all has been considered and demands & merits observation. If this be called obscurity, let it be remembered tis such a one as is complaisant to the Reader: not that vicious obscurity, which proceeds from a muddled head" (*Notebooks*, vol. 1, no. 276). In a similar way he defends his "Sonnet, Composed on a Journey Homeward" in a letter to Thelwall in 1796: "My first *Sonnet is obscure*; but you ought to distinguish between obscurity residing in the uncommonness of the thought, and that which proceeds from thoughts unconnected & language not adapted to the expression of them. When you *do* find out the meaning of my poetry, can you . . . alter the language so as to make it more perspicuous—the thought remaining the same?"[28] Here the simple differentiation of two meanings for a single word allows Coleridge to fashion an effective tool for literary judgments. The political context is clearly an ingredient in that term, and the political connotations, present in Coleridge's exaggerated defense of the term, indeed charge that word *obscurity* with a special social resonance.

If obscurity is tangentially related to egotism in poetry and politics, the reader's duty that Coleridge refers to in the comment on his sonnet suggests the second of his two key words, *benevolence*. As it does for his eighteenth-century predecessors like Shaftesbury, benevolence acquires a special importance for Coleridge, since it embraces a number of Hartleian notions about fellow feeling, sympathy, human compassion, moral goodness, and duty. Like *egotism*, therefore, *benevolence* is a multifaceted term that resounds with many connotations that are ultimately organized by Coleridge according to their social and political value. Woodring notes that in Coleridge's early poetry the most significant words "are *gentle, calm, mild*. Next after nostalgia the motif most recurring is pity, sometimes as compassion, sympathy, or benevolence. The great subversive marriage of ideas in the second half of the eighteenth century was that of liberty with pity, for charity thereby claimed a superiority to law

and established justice."[29]And in *The Watchman* Coleridge
defines duties and rights in a manner that is fundamentally
grounded on principles of a humanistic love and kindness,
mixing Hartley and Godwin: "Those duties are called DU-
TIES which we exercise toward others; those duties are called
RIGHTS which we exercise in favor of ourselves. It is the
DUTY of each individual to aim at producing the greatest
possible happiness to the whole: and as the happiness of
the whole is made up of its parts, it is the RIGHT of each
individual to enjoy every pleasure which does not injure
himself, nor lessen nor render insecure the enjoyments of
others" (*Watchman*, p. 122n). The private affections direct
an individual to his rights and duties, and consequently private benevolence leads to universal benevolence and social
amelioration:

> The searcher after Truth must love and be beloved, for
> general Benevolence is a necessary motive to constancy
> of pursuit; and this general Benevolence is begotten and
> rendered permanent by social and domestic affections.
> Let us beware that proved Philosophy, which affects to
> inculcate Philanthropy while it denounces every home-
> born feeling, by which it is produced and nurtured. The
> paternal and filial duties discipline the Heart and pre-
> pare it for the love of all Mankind. The intensity of pri-
> vate attachments encourages, not prevents, universal
> Benevolence. (*Lectures 1795*, p. 46)

The way this benevolence and the ideas associated with it
enter Coleridge's literary criticism is most bluntly suggested
by a passage describing the writings and lectures of John
Thelwall. Indeed Thelwall's political work is obviously not
literature, but its emphasis on honest feelings and the kind
heart above all else is a refrain that echoes through much of
Coleridge's literary commentary. "The feelings of men are

always founded in truth," Coleridge says; "the modes of expressing them may lead to the most abhorred excesses. Yet still they are originally right: they teach men that something is wanting, something which he ought to have" (*Lectures 1795*, p. 129). About poetry specifically he writes in 1796 "that the most interesting passages in all writings are those in which the author develops his own feelings. The sweet voice of Cona [Ossian] never sounds so sweetly as when it speaks of itself; and I should almost suspect that man of an unkindly heart, who could read the opening of the third book of Paradise Lost without peculiar emotion. By a law of our own nature, he who labours under a strong feeling is impelled to seek for sympathy; but a poet's feelings are all strong. . . . Akenside therefore speaks with philosophical accuracy when he classes Love and Poetry, as producing the same effects."[30] Here as often during these years, Coleridge's critical methodology and language transforms the poem into a measure of the writer's personal sympathies: whether the key critical term is *benevolence, feeling, good,* or a related expression, it serves primarily to describe the value of the poem in terms of the humanistic potential of the writer. Coleridge accordingly hails Sir Thomas Browne in 1802 as "an affectionate visionary" whose work presents "a sweet exhibition of character and passion, and not . . . an expression, or investigation, of positive truth."[31] And, in a notebook jotting, he evaluates George Dyer's poetry in terms of the poet's own benevolent personality: "George Dyer's Character—moral (not intellectual) Truth & benevolence struggling" (*Notebooks,* vol. 1, no. 487). Later, when Coleridge's extraliterary concerns would move more radically into psychology, it is significant that he reevaluates Dyer with a psychological language that finds benevolence an insufficient attribute in a poet, thus relegating Dyer to the second rank.

Benevolent feeling is so important to Coleridge in these

early years, though, that its presence could override nearly any other fault in a poet. Coleridge comments on Charles Lloyd's sonnet "My Bible! Scarcely Dare I Open Thee!": "This is a very rough-cast Sonnet; but the beauty & goodness of the sentiments redeem it from its faults & make it dear to the good" (*Notebooks*, vol. 1, no. 487n). Kathleen Coburn hence accurately observes in Coleridge's and Lamb's favorable reaction to Dyer, "The benevolence of their eccentric friend was considered greater than his intellectual acumen,"[32] a point that Coleridge's annotations on the preface of Dyer's *Poems* confirms. Somewhat ironically Coleridge implies here that the benevolent Dyer does not fully understand the role of benevolent feeling in poetry. Objecting to a number of Dyer's comments, Coleridge claims, "My benevolent friend seems not to have made an obvious distinction between end and means. The poet *must* always aim at pleasure as his specific *means*; but . . . all ought to aim at something nobler as their end—viz.—to cultivate and predispose the heart of the reader."[33]

What Dyer fails to grasp is that benevolence relates also to the effect of poetry. In the 1794 version of a sonnet to Bowles, Coleridge describes what he believes should be the effect of great poetry:

> My heart has thank'd thee, Bowles! for those soft
>   strains,
> That, on the still air floating, tremblingly
> Wak'd in me Fancy, Love, and Sympathy!
> For hence, not callous to a Brother's pains
>
> Thro' Youth's gay prime and thornless paths I went;
> And, when the *darker* day of life began,
> And I did roam, a thought-bewilder'd man!
> The kindred Lays an healing solace lent.[34]

Poetry, that is, educates and cultivates the reader's affections and feelings, and, in doing so, unites two crucial social concepts for Coleridge: Hartley's notion of the primacy of affections in benevolent action and Godwin's plan for the improvement of society through the schematic education of all men and women. Following Hartley, Coleridge writes, "The ardour of private Attachments makes Philanthropy a necessary *habit* of the Soul,"[35] and Hartley's private affections thus begin to acquire larger political significance. Moreover, since personal affections are formed by one's environment and social situation, Godwin's behavioristic theories about education are also valuable. An early note merges the two ideas (Rousseau substituting for Godwin):

> We know too well, that it is not the mere notation however clear that restrains or impels us; but the feelings habitually connected with that notion. The drunkard is convinced that his Drams are poison yet he takes them. For once that a deep conviction is the parent of a Habit, a Habit is an 100 times the parent of the conviction. Hence the immense importance of Education i.e. *training up*. Hence the sophistry may be shewn of Rousseau's Plan of Education in which an intellectual conviction is always to precede the appropriate action. Education is to man what the transmission of Instinct is to animals—entwines Thought with the living Substance, the nerves of sensation, the organ of soul, the muscles of motion, and this, finally, with the *Will*—the total soul energises, unique and unific.[36]

The best poetry always educates in this way, so that the reader's affections are nurtured and he becomes a more sympathetic and sensitive citizen, social benevolence springing from this cultivation of affection into sympathy. "Sympathy the Poet alone can excite," Coleridge says, "any Dabbler in stories can excite Pity" (*Notebooks*, vol. 1, no. 957). And in the first preface to his 1796 poems, he returns continually to poetry's power to instruct the emotions in sympathy and sorrow. "The communicativeness of our nature leads us to describe our own sorrows," he asserts. "In the endeavor to describe them intellectual activity is exerted; and from intellectual activity there results a pleasure, which is gradually associated, and mingles as a corrective, with the painful subject of the description." This private experience in turn has public ramifications, he continues, since the public is "but a term for a number of scattered individuals . . . of whom as many will be interested in these sorrows as have experienced the same or similar."[37] In this way Coleridge's poems can claim a powerful social significance, one which Coleridge more or less creates for them through a critical preface which employs a language constantly directed towards the sphere of social action.

Finally, this same political morality of educating sensibilities, this mixture of Hartley and Godwin embodied in the language of feelings, benevolence, and "the heart," accounts for one of Coleridge's loudest criticisms of *The Monk*, here pertaining to Ambrosio, the main character. Lewis, Coleridge says, fails to understand the way feeling is nurtured and depraved, and so shows great "ignorance of the human heart in the management of the principal character. The wisdom and goodness of providence have ordered that the tendency of vicious actions to deprave the heart of the perpetrator, should diminish in proportion to the greatness of the temptations." Moreover, in the same review Coleridge uses a similar argument and the same language of feeling in one of his most incisive critical observations, the supernatural being here primarily a moral and political question, not the psychological problem it becomes a number of years later:

The romance-writer possesses an unlimited power over situations; but he must scrupulously make his characters act in congruity with them. Let him work *physical* wonders only, and we will be content to *dream* with him for awhile; but the first moral miracle he attempts, he disgusts and awakens us. . . . [These are events] not preternatural, but contrary to nature. The extent of the powers that may exist, we can never ascertain; and therefore we feel no great difficulty in yielding a temporary belief in any, the strangest, situation of *things*. But that situation once conceived, how beings like ourselves would feel and act in it, our own feelings sufficiently instruct us; and we instantly reject the clumsy fiction that does not harmonise with them.[38]

The wellspring for many of these ideas about the politics of benevolence and the relation between natural feeling and political morality is clearly Rousseau, who in his *Discourse on the Origin of Inequality* suggests an original state of primitive benevolence, and who argues in other works like *The Social Contract* for a harmonious society based on man's natural feeling and sensibility. Rousseau's impact on Coleridge can be seen especially in his early years, when he and Southey dreamed of a pantosocratic paradise. Yet Coleridge gradually adjusts Rousseau's ideas to his own notions of benevolence, and eventually develops a more private and dynamic theory of the social contract. In one marginal note he writes, "Reflect on an original Social contract, as an *incident*, or historical *fact*: and its gross improbability: not to say impossibility, will stare you in the Face. But an ever originating Social Contract *is* an Idea, which exists and works continually and efficaciously in the Moral Being of every free Citizen, tho' in the greater number unconsciously or with a dimmed and confused consciousness."[39] Equally political, Coleridge and Rousseau's theories rely on the inherent goodness or benevolence of each individual, and, at least in his early years, Coleridge locates the source of this benevolence in a primitive, uncorrupted innocence, associated with the Romantic ideal of nature, agriculture, and political liberty: "Liberty—the Solitude free & natural, the Nature unmanacled & solitary, the Liberty natural & solitary" (Notebooks, vol. 1, no. 1504). Opposed to this natural innocence is the corruption of the city, the chicanery of politics, and the decadence of aristocrats, making the Romantic idealization of nature a decidedly political strategy. Discussing the ancient Germans in The Watchman, for example, Coleridge launches a thinly disguised attack on contemporary British society "that only can with propriety be stiled refinement, which, by the strengthening of the intellect, purifies the manners. All else enervates and depraves. If a mind skilled in the routine of etiquette, and the nothingness of politesse, and a body enfeebled by the delicate languor of fashion, constitute refinement, I must turn to contemplate the dignity of woman in the tent of a barbarian" (p. 90).

Like the rest of his politics, many of these youthful notions about innate goodness and the savage state would alter considerably as he matured. Even in these early years, he never embraces the peasant as enthusiastically as does Wordsworth, who sometimes seems to consecrate a person simply for being poor and ragged. "A curious & more than curious fact," Coleridge writes, is "that when the country does not benefit, it depraves" (Notebooks, vol. 1, no. 1553). Moreover, the noble peasant is often simply boring: "Adam Smith's arguments on the superiority of Rustics false. . . . Farmers talk always of their own occupations" (no. 735). The guidelines of civilization are always an important requisite for Coleridge, and if the savage state is a healty alternative to a degenerate society, this must be distinguished from the barbaric state, which is as dangerous as any despotism: "Barbarism [as distinguished from] Savage State is the Effect or Result of Moral Corruption, False Religion, Priestcraft and Despotism, whether it be the Despotism of one, of few, or of the Many, i.e. whether it be a monarchical, an aristocratical or a democratical Despotism. It (Barbarism, I mean) consists in the absence of the means of National and individual Progression by the accumulation of Knowledge and Experience from age to age."[40]

Nonetheless, when he writes about literature, Coleridge follows Wordsworth's idealization of the benevolent peasant much more closely than is often acknowledged.[41] At his worst, Coleridge can unintentionally parody Wordsworth's defense of a rustic language and subjects, and make statements like this rather ridiculous comparison of the poet and the honest farmer who differ only in their rewards: "The Husbandman puts his seed in the Ground & the Goodness, Power, & Wisdom of God have pledged themselves, that he shall have Bread, and Health, & Quietness in return for Industry, & Simplicity of Wants, & Innocence. The *Author* scatters his seed—with aching head, and wasted Health, & all the heart leapings of Anxiety—& the Folly, the Vices, & the Fickleness of Man promise Printers' Bills & the Debtors' Side of Newgate, as full and sufficient Payment."[42] A more interesting and more obviously political use of this Rousseauistic perception, though, is a 1799 notebook entry on a ballad in Percy's *Reliques*, "Babes in the Wood." "Praise of Poetry—vinedresser—compare the author of the Babes in the wood with Bounaparte [*sic*]" (*Notebooks*, vol. 1, no. 620). As Coburn explains in her annotation to this remark, Coleridge is here praising this poem as "an example of the power and innocence and simplicity in poetry compared with the destructive power of men of action like Bonaparte." The comment is rich, primarily because of the complex political resonances it establishes by setting Rousseau's vision against the product of that vision as it appeared on the political scene years later.

Coleridge's most consistent use of natural innocence and the beauty of savagery in his literary criticism, however, appears in *The Watchman*, which is a particularly interesting work because it demonstrates how basic mechanical decisions like the selection and positioning of poetry in a journal can become effective political commentary. Here, Coleridge invariably chooses either poems with overt political meaning or poems like John Logan's "The Braes of Yarrow," whose rustic virtues (the poem is "simple, deeply pathetic, and even sublime") identify it with democratic politics (*Watchman*, p. 106). Moreover, positioning a poem like Logan's just before a description of the catastrophes of the present war (a strategy Coleridge frequently employs in *The Watchman*) creates a tension which acts as a retroactive commentary on the poem: Pitt and his aristocratic ministry, in other words, have perpetrated a brutal and inhuman war on the simple and sensitive lower class represented by Logan's poem.

Three other examples from *The Watchman* illustrate these same techniques nicely and show how he supplements them with a powerfully connotative language that activates the political meaning sometimes latent in the literature and sometimes forced on it. In the first example, Coleridge analyzes Beddoes's "Essay on Pitt" in which Beddoes decries the "miseries of the poor in the country, and of the poor in the towns" (p. 310), miseries Pitt's war created. Following this article is an account of Louis de Boissy, a French dramatist before the Revolution who nearly died of starvation. Comparing Boissy with Otway, Collins, and Chatterton, Coleridge remarks that Boissy, "in addition to great intellectual ability, possessed the virtues of Industry and Temperance"—rustic uncorrupted virtues—"yet his works produced him fame only. He laboured incessantly for uncertain bread" (p. 314). Thus, together, the two essays make it clear that political and social injustice attacks merit and honest virtue in the poet as well as in the peasant, uniting them in their suffering and their struggle to preserve a basic moral integrity. Later in a brief criticism of Beddoes's novel, *The History of Isaac Jenkins*, Coleridge similarly praises the simple, direct style of Beddoes's writing, and, using language which duplicates his contrast of the idyllic, Republican nature and the corrupted Tory city, he compares the novel with an episode in Sterne's *Tristram Shandy*; according to Coleridge, *The History of Isaac Jenkins* is "a tale in every respect superior to Stern's Le Fevre, as the vivid images of nature to the creatures of an eccentric imagination, as the feelings of active benevolence to the effusions of artificial sensibility" (p. 313).

Finally, in the same issue Coleridge includes three Esthonian Ballads to which he adds a prefatory explication which forces the reader to view these primitive poems in the context of Rousseauistic politics:

> The Poetry, which we have yet seen, of savage nations, present us with descriptions of manners, totally dissimilar to our own, and those rude energies of mind which dignify the human animal. . . . The following specimens of a Sclavonian nation are less elevated, but perhaps more interesting. They are the effusions of a people uncivilized themselves, yet groaning beneath the oppressions of civilized society. The Esthonians, a few of whose popular ballads we are about to give our readers, inhabit the upper regions of the Gulf of Finland: they are subject to the Germans, and never did human beings experience more cruel masters. The two latter ballads might be sung with feeling, and I fear, much truth by our own peasants. (p. 316)

Coleridge's emphasis on the "natural" with its suggestions of a benevolent and harmonious society is perhaps even more subtly present in a series of critical articles on four Gothic novels which Coleridge wrote for the *Critical Review* between 1794 and 1798. Reviewing Radcliffe's *The Italian*, he writes: "It was not difficult to forsee that the *modern romance*, even supported by the skill of the most ingenious of its votaries, would soon experience the fate of every attempt to please by what is unnatural, and by a departure from the observance of real life, which has placed the work of Fielding, Smollet, and some other writers, among the permanent sources of amusement."[43] Clearly, the natural world implied here is a variation on the primitive world of savages and peasants which served him in *The Watchman*. Yet the meaning is much the same, simply broadened to include other parts of the spectrum of nature. In both cases, the natural world is opposed to a sophisticated but effete society whose death was signaled by the French Revolution. A short note on Mary Robinson's *Hubert de Sevrac*, therefore, first mildly approves of certain romantic scenes, but then warns readers "that this taste is declining, and that real life and manners will soon assert their claims."[44] And, in an unfriendly review of *The Monk*, Coleridge announces the end of this decadent kind of literature with language which reflects, it seems, a sated and somewhat decadent European society:

> The horrible and the preternatural have usually seized on the popular taste, at the rise and decline of literature. Most powerful stimulants, they can never be required except by the torpor of an unawakened, or the languor of an exhausted appetite. The same phaenomenon, therefore, which we hail as a favourable omen in the belles lettres of Germany, impresses a degree of gloom in the compositions of our own countrymen. We trust, however, that satiety will banish what good sense should have prevented; and that, wearied with fiends, incomprehensible characters, with shrieks, murders, and sub-

terraneous dungeons, the public will learn, by the multitude of the manufacturers, with how little expense of thought or imagination this species of composition is manufactured.[45]

Notably (in the last sentence) this description of romance writers as manufacturers concludes its attack by equating these authors with a political group, the rising middle-class industrialists, for whom Coleridge had little regard and few good expectations. The main crime against the natural world in these novels, though, is their dependence on superstitions, a word that has two meanings for Coleridge, meanings which are both fraught with political significance and which, like egotism and obscurity, receive their explicit moral and political force from the semantic distinction that Coleridge posits and uses in his criticism. On the one hand, superstition is connected with a political tyranny built on a religion of mystery and fear. In his first lecture on revealed religion Coleridge discusses this kind of superstition, and acutely equates it with an atheistic materialism, since both worship dark mysteries, one in nature, the other in religion; hence, Godwin and Holcraft are as disagreeable as the reactionary Bench of Bishops. On the other hand, superstition can be beneficial—religiously and politically. Coleridge copies this passage from Henry More's *An Antidote against Atheism*: "A contemptuous misbelief of such like narrations concerning *Spirits*, & an endeavor of making them all ridiculous & incredible, is a dangerous prelude to atheism itself, or else a more close & crafty profession and insinuation of it. For assuredly that saying is not more true in Politics, *No Bishop, no King*; than this is in Metaphysics, *No Spirit, no God*" (Notebooks, vol. I, no. 1000G). Yet Coleridge qualifies More's statement significantly by suggesting that superstition is primarily useful for the uneducated masses, who are not always intellectually capable of discovering religious truth through reason (no. 243). In a passage that leaves no doubt about the political import of superstition Coleridge argues,

> The truth seems to be, that Superstition is unfavorable to civil freedom then only, when it teaches sensuality, . . . or when it is in alliance with power and avarice. . . . In all other cases, to forego, even in solitude, the high pleasures which the human mind receives from the free exertion of its faculties, through the dread of an invisible spectator or the hope of a future reward, implies so great a conquest over the tyranny of the present impulse, and so large a power of self-government, that whoever is conscious of it, will be grateful for the existence of an external government no farther than as it protects him from the attacks of others. (*Watchman*, p. 12)

Religion and superstition, in Colmer's words, "by directing the mind to the thought of an after life teaches a self-discipline and self-government that make the individual critical of all forms of public misgovernment, particularly of measures that interfere with the liberty of the individual."[46]

These two meanings for superstition, used as differentiated codes, are especially important, I believe, for an understanding of what would otherwise be inconsistent criticisms of the Gothic romances and whimsical vacillation between defending and attacking terror in art. In his review of *The Mysteries of Udolpho*, Coleridge praises Mrs. Radcliffe's vision "Of horror, . . . and thrilling fears," and admires the mysterious terrors that are "continually exciting in the mind the idea of a supernatural appearance, keeping us, as it were, upon the edge and confines of the world of the spirits, and yet are ingeniously explained by familiar causes."[47] Similarly, he denounces Johnson's and Wharton's belief in stage restraint as "hysterical Humanité," and intends to "reprobate this notion" of not allowing "too horrid things like Gloucester's eyes on stage" (*Notebooks*, vol. 1, no. 127). (It is interesting that in his later Shakespearean criticism, operating with more staid politics, he reverses this decision.) The reasons for these positive evaluations of terror and the supernatural are unmistakable. It is obvious throughout the reviews that Coleridge sees the novel as a working-class amusement; hence the superstition in these works is a healthy stimulus, both religiously and politically, for an uneducated audience. Writing to Thelwall about his childhood and the development of his then highly impressionable mind, Coleridge explains this power: "Should children be permitted to read Romances, & Relations of Giants & Magicians, & Genii?—I know all that has been said against it; but I have formed my faith in the affirmative.—I know no other way of giving the mind a love of 'the Great,' & 'the Whole.'"[48]

Conversely, Coleridge lambastes the kind of superstition he finds in *The Monk*, and if from a literary point of view this appears inconsistent, politically it is not. As applied to *The Monk* superstition refers to a sensuality which, as he observes in *The Watchman*, "is an alliance with power" (p. 12). It neither elevates the reader nor inspires religious awe, as does most of Mrs. Radcliffe's fiction. Thus Coleridge lashes out with an angry description of sensual superstition.

> Mildness of censure would here be criminally misplaced, and silence would make us accomplices. Not without reluctance then, but in full conviction that we are performing a duty, we declare it to be our opinion, that the Monk is a romance, which if a parent saw in the hands of a son or daughter, he might reasonably turn pale. The temptations of Ambrosio are described with libidinous minuteness. . . . The shameless harlotry of Matilda, and the trembling innocence of Antonia, are seized with

> equal avidity, as vehicles of the most voluptuous images. . . . [Lewis furnishes] a *mormo* for children, a poison for youth, and a provocative for the debauchee. Tales of enchantments and witchcraft can never be *useful*: our author has contrived to make them *pernicious*, by blending, with an irreverent negligence, all that is most awfully true in religion with all that is most ridiculously absurd in superstition.[49]

Superstition and imaginative terrors should be redemptive; they should liberate readers from the burden of the physical and the demands of the political in order that their political and moral decisions will be untrammeled. *The Monk*, however, creates a terror that is predominantly physical and, instead of freeing the reader, buries him further in the ugliness of the physical world. Superstitious fears should ultimately give the pleasure of release and spiritual awe. In *The Monk*, the devices of terror all pertain to the physical world and therefore simply foment the callow, working-class reader's fear of the physical. *The Monk* is a world without any redemptive imagination, and the displeasure in reading it signals its failure as conscientious art:

> The sufferings which he describes are so frightful and intolerable, that we break with abruptness from the delusion, and indignantly suspect the man of a species of brutality, who could find a pleasure in wantonly imagining them. . . . The merit of the novellist is in proportion (not simply to the effect, but,) to the *pleasurable* effect which he produces. Situations of torment, and images of naked horror, are easily conceived; and a writer in whose works they abound, deserves our gratitude almost equally with him who should drag us by way of sport through a military hospital, or force us to sit at the dissecting table of a natural philosopher. To trace the

nice boundaries, beyond which terror and sympathy are deserted by the pleasurable emotions,—to reach those limits, yet never to pass them—hic labor, hic opus est [sic].[50]

As in most of Coleridge's political and moral criticism of literature, in this last passage, Coleridge's language pushes through the text to the citizen behind it. A dangerously sensual projection of an author's imagination in itself, The Monk becomes even more appalling for Coleridge because the author is a member of Parliament: "Nor must it be forgotten that the author is a man of rank and fortune.—yes! the author of the Monk signs himself a LEGISLATOR!—We stare and tremble."[51] Coleridge could not have known that Mathew Lewis was the author. But when his name was disclosed, Coleridge's fears about the writer's political power would have appeared justified, since the author of The Monk was not only a Tory member of the House of Commons but a former official in the War Office, a Jamaican slave owner, and diametrically opposite Coleridge's politics in nearly every way.

Written near the conclusion of his most fervid political years, Coleridge's reviews of The Monk and the three other romances represent sometimes his most overt and sometimes his subtlest use of a political language to infuse literature with a moral and social significance. At the same time, though, they show new interests already seeping into his literary criticism. 1798 was the year of disillusionment for Coleridge and other young revolutionaries who had pinned their political hopes on France: Napoleon's invasion of Switzerland and the deposition of the Spanish government sobered Coleridge and his comrades and led to major reassessments of their politics. Though he would never completely free himself from the maelstrom of politics, his involvement would become increasingly more oblique. Never again would

73

his literary criticism be so pervasively influenced by solid political issues like the personalities of Pitt and Napoleon, slavery, the education of the poor, the two Sedition Bills, the rights of citizens, and the role of benevolence in the amelioration of society. In his last years politics would be overshadowed by theology, while at the turn of the century Coleridge would be reworking Hartley's psychology and, with more conviction, locating the source of social improvement in the mind of the individual. In fact, in these early reviews, psychology is already entering Coleridge's reading and criticism, when, for instance, he examines how the reader's curiosity operates in *The Monk* and *The Mysteries of Udolpho* and how "the perception of *difficulty* surmounted" is a crucial ingredient in a good romance. As he learned to adapt this psychological language to literature, his literary criticism would obviously become more sophisticated. Yet the directness and often brilliance of his early criticism and notes on literature will always make this youthful work valuable in its own right. In these early years, Coleridge was able to actuate literature, to make it immediately relevant to the pressures of politics around him, not in the vulgar manner that clumsy social critics are often guilty of, but by finding and using terms and a language which functioned well for both politics and literature. His political terms could accommodate without distorting, provide insights that were original without straining the boundaries of literature. More important, perhaps, the political language in his literary notes and essays makes literature echo with a concrete political meaning that, while allowing the poet to stay off the barriers, forces him out of the drawing rooms of the eighteenth century.

CHAPTER THREE

Naturalization and Psychology in Coleridge's Shakespeare Criticism, 1800–1812

The only nomenclature of criticism should be the classification of the faculties of the mind, how they are placed, how they are subordinate, whether they do or do not appeal to the worthy feelings of our nature. False criticism is created by ignorance, light removes it; as the croaking of frogs in a ditch is silenced by a candle.

COLERIDGE,
Shakespearean Criticism, 1813

IN 1811 COLERIDGE NOTES that the capricious Romeo's fluctuating affections early in Shakespeare's play are explained by a fundamental "law of the mind" which Coleridge "shall hereafter be able to make intelligible, and which would not only justify Shakespeare, but show an analogy to all his other characters."[1] The announcement is, of course, no surprise to a modern student of Coleridge, since today Coleridge is somewhat notorious for his practice of literary naturalization—a popular critical method at the turn of the eighteenth century whereby a critic analyzes and describes a fictional character as if he or she had the same emotional and psychological complexities as a real person. Romeo's case, in other words, is just one of many in which Coleridge insists on the commensurability of the psychological theories of his day and the psychological realities of the characters he studies and in which he exaggerates (or sometimes reduces) the complexities of those characters accordingly.

Yet, accurate as this summary is, it underestimates the extent to which psychology and psychological naturalization permeates Coleridge's literary criticism. Readers commonly note how Coleridge "overreads" Shakespeare's characters, assigning features to their personalities which would be difficult to locate in the text itself. But as recent schools of structuralist critics have made clear, naturalization includes much more than character analysis, and overreading a text can involve many other types of productive reading. Whereas at the beginning of the nineteenth century *naturalization* referred exclusively to the practice of interpreting a character so that he or she became more real than fictional, for the structuralist it now describes a variety of reading practices in which any feature of a primary text is recuperated in terms of one of the reader-critic's cultural interpretive codes (contemporary psychology being one of these codes). The structuralist's use of the term would then embrace the Romantic definition, since the psychologizing of dramatic characters would be just one of many ways—obviously the favorite way—that a Romantic reader could make sense of a text. That Coleridge uses psychology to naturalize Shakespeare's plays means therefore that what most nearly approximates a language of psychology controls many features of the text besides character, and that his formal criticism, for instance, has far less to do with the objective characteristics of drama than with complex psychological models based on Coleridge's studies of dreams and audience response. Further, it is the psychological language itself, not its connection with Coleridge's metaphysics, that requires special attention, since it is this language, used as literary criticism, that produces the peculiar and often brilliant psychological meanings Coleridge gives to Shakespeare's plays. Language is not an innocent instrument; "words are no Passive Tools."[2] And examining the historical and personal connotations of a primarily psychological term like *rationalized dream* becomes an important and revealing way of illustrating how Coleridge actively makes meaning with the language he uses and how the connotative consistency of that language provides a unity to a literary criticism at times disturbingly independent of the literature it criticizes. A "subtle-souled psychologist" by nature, Coleridge attempts to breathe a complex life into literary texts and fictional characters with the psychological language he uses, a life not necessarily more complex than the lives and texts the artist creates, but certainly idiosyncratic in its dependence on Coleridge's individual notions of psychological complexity and verisimilitude. Indeed, because of these idiosyncracies and complexities, Coleridge's literary criticism during this period often seems more diffuse than ever, the language of psychology literally interwoven or interpolated into the literary criticism, so that it becomes extremely difficult to say where one assimilates the other. For the sake of clarity, therefore, I will concentrate here on Coleridge's naturalization of literary characters according to the psychological models he develops within the associational tradition, and then demonstrate how this extraliterary model and its discourse allows Coleridge to shift logically from character analyses to analyses of dramatic form, where his central terms—*passion, dream, interest,* and *curiosity*—combine to form a surprisingly coherent and effective discourse for literary criticism. Reading literature by means of these interpretive keys, Coleridge leaves little doubt that literature manifests the same mysterious activity that contemporary psychology was discovering in the human mind.

THERE ARE SOME ESPECIALLY GOOD EXAMPLES of the standard naturalization process in Coleridge's Shakespeare criticism, examples which most readers notice and at which Coleridge's own contemporaries often raised eyebrows. Most egregiously, in what are clearly peculiar Coleridgean readings, he idealizes Shakespeare's women to a point where they are nearly unrecognizable. Noting the "reverence in which he [Shakespeare] holds women," Coleridge continually defends the perfection and angelic virtue of Shakespeare's females. Writing about *Measure for Measure,* he accordingly makes the somewhat puzzling remark that the "pardon and marriage of Angela not merely baffles the strong indignant claim of justice . . . but it is likewise degrading to the character of woman" (*Shakespearean Criticism*, 1 : 102). Often this chivalric standard—which it seems Coleridge felt was very realistic—does not greatly diminish his usual critical acumen, although many of Shakespeare's most famous women suffer gross misunderstanding because of it. Characters like Goneril and Regan, for instance, seem to resist the model to such an extent that applying it to them appears almost ludicrous. And Coleridge clearly is struggling when he tries to show the supposed idolization of femininity at work in Lady Macbeth, one of Shakespeare's least perfect women. In a sophisticated psychological maneuver Coleridge relies on his conception of the will to help explain Lady Macbeth's actions, arguing that she is voluntarily bad but involuntarily good as her feminine virtue invariably asserts itself against her will:

> So far is the woman from being dead within her, that her sex occasionally betrays itself in the very moment of dark and bloodly imagination. A passage where she alludes to "plucking her nipple from the boneless gums of her infant," though usually thought to prove a merciless and unwomanly nature, proves the direct opposite: she brings it as the most solemn enforcement to Macbeth of the solemnity of his promise to undertake the plot against Duncan. Had *she* so sworn, she would have done that which was most horrible to her feelings, rather than break the oath; and as the most horrible act which it was possible for imagination to conceive, as that which was most revolting to her own feelings, she alludes to the destruction of her infant, while in the act of sucking at her breast. Had she regarded this with savage indifference there would have been no force in this appeal; but her very allusion to it, and purpose in this appeal, shows

that she considered no tie as tender as that which connected her with her babe. (2:221)

Perhaps even better known are Coleridge's interpretations
of Shakespeare's villains. Often these readings contain some
of his best criticism, and, like his analysis of Lady Macbeth,
the stubbornness of the reading could without too much
difficulty be defended as a perceptive, close reading of the
text. To be sure, seeing Claudius as part victim or justifying
Edmund's actions in *King Lear* are not really far-fetched interpretations but a result of the complexity in the characters
that many recent Shakespearean critics have acknowledged.
Coleridge's special touch is undoubtedly present in his readings when, for instance, he so obtrusively employs his celebrated distinction between moral feeling and intellect as a
critical touchstone for explaining the behavior of these villains.[3] But these interpretations often ring true, and their attraction then comes from their accuracy, not their idiosyn-
cracy. When this same language is used in other instances,
however, it creates some embarrassing moments in Coleridge's criticism. Such a case is his description of Falstaff,
whom he places in a category with amoral intellects like
Richard III and Iago. Here the model and terminology with
which he attempts to explain Falstaff's character seem a particularly unnatural Procrustean bed that makes Falstaff more
Coleridge's than Shakespeare's. And the most outstanding
feature of this productively aberrant reading is probably Coleridge's failure to apprehend the humor in Falstaff's character.
Coleridge writes,

> Falstaff was no coward, but pretended to be one merely
> for the sake of trying experiments on the credulity of
> mankind: he was a liar with the same object, and not
> because he loved falsehood for itself. He was a man of

such preeminent abilities, as to give him a profound con-
tempt for all those by whom he was usually surrounded,
and to lead to a determination on his part, in spite of their
fancied superiority, to make them his tools and dupes. He
knew, however low he descended, that his own talents
would raise him from any difficulty. While he was
thought to be the greatest rogue, thief, and liar, he still
had that about him not only respectable, but absolutely
necessary to his companions. It was in characters of
complete moral depravity, but of first-rate wit and talents, that Shakespeare delighted. (2:26)

Similarly, Coleridge makes the curious statement that "there
is no character in Shakespeare in which envy is pourtrayed,
with one solitary exception—Cassius" (2:110). In each of
these last cases, Coleridge's comments can only be called
very singular readings, explainable only in terms of a critical terminology that prevents him from describing Shakespeare's text accurately. They are, in short, naturalized readings that, instead of inflating the primary material, fail to
accommodate and understand the true dimensions of that
material.

Though many of these odd readings in Coleridge's criticism have been noted before, my study adds, I believe, an
important emphasis that stresses the pervasive and constitutive presence of psychological language in Coleridge's Shakespearean criticism (some expressions as well known as *will*
and *illusion* but more particularly overlooked terms like *curiosity* and *passion*), and illustrates the interdependence of
these terms in Coleridge's psychological framework. Coleridge's sometimes odd readings, in short, do not result from
an inability to read and criticize properly but from the limitations and connotations of a critical language that receives
its unity and definition from a discourse outside literature
which is then applied to literature. It is easy to disregard the

productive capacity of this language primarily because the terms and insights provided by it have weathered so many years of use and remain part of our own critical vocabulary. We therefore commonly assign terms like *passion* and *curiosity* neutral or literary meanings that are more ours than Coleridge's (we too tend to naturalize language), and thus miss the very specific connotations of his literary criticism and the way it roots its meaning firmly in his conception of what is psychologically true. A second reason that this productive capacity in Coleridge's Shakespeare criticism is frequently overlooked, moreover, is quite simply that Shakespeare's character-oriented plays seem to demand a psychological language such as Coleridge's in order to encompass and describe the extraordinary minds that are the center of the dramatic action. Rather than undermining the idea of productivity in Coleridge's psychological criticism, however, this coincidence of material and interpretation suggests that all criticism, and certainly Coleridge's, depends to some extent on begging its questions, the choice of a literary subject becoming a product of the controlling language. Thus Shakespeare's characters will naturally figure less prominently in Coleridge's criticism as his interest in psychology wanes.

In his *Structuralist Poetics*, Jonathan Culler helps elucidate some of these questions by suggesting how literary characters are read and understood. When we read, Culler says, the process of selecting and organizing the character-semes, the units of meaning for a character,

> is governed by an ideology of character, implicit models of psychological coherence which indicate what sorts of things are possible as character traits, how these traits can coexist and form wholes, or at least which traits coexist without difficulty and which are necessarily opposed in ways that produce tension and ambiguity. To a

certain extent, of course, these notions are drawn from non-literary experience. . . . As soon as the basic outline of a character begins to emerge in the process of readings, one can call upon any of the languages developed for the study of human behaviour and begin to structure the text in those terms. As Barthes emphasizes, the seme is only a point of departure, an avenue of meaning; one cannot say what lies at the end of the road—"everything depends on the level at which one halts the process of naming."[4]

I am of course drawing attention to those "non-literary experiences" and saying that "models of psychological coherence"—Coleridge's favorite models during his middle years —are just one type of model that a reader may use to elicit a character's meaning. (Marxists have shown that economic models offer at least one other way in which characters cohere.) Moreover, I am claiming that the selection and organization of character-semes by a reader-critic necessarily involves a kind of translation, or that the organization itself is by its nature a translation process.

This naturalization as translation process is most dramatically illustrated in Coleridge's poem "Religious Musings," where, for instance, in one of his footnotes Coleridge glosses a poetic passage with a Hartleyan explanation. Less overtly the same process operates in his Shakespeare criticism, where the terms and analyses are acknowledged by most critics—perhaps with too little care for the implications—as fundamentally psychological. Coleridge's distinctions between meditation and observation, moral feeling and willful intellect, or fancy and imagination are at this period in his life obviously psychological notions. Allen Tate's remarks are typical of the superficial and vague way many readers understand these terms: "The distinction between Fancy and Imagination is ultimately a psychological one: he discusses the problem in terms of separate faculties, and the objective poetic properties, presumably resulting from the rise of these, are never defined, but are given only occasional illustration."[5] Drawing attention to finer linguistic distinctions, less obtrusive psychological terms, and the historical connotations of this language, however, helps correct these loose summaries of Coleridge's criticism and in addition challenges some shaky common presuppositions. M. M. Badawi's *Coleridge: Critic of Shakespeare*, for instance, is a sound and informative study, and I often rely on some of its findings. But it illustrates the danger of a common tendency to treat Coleridge's criticism, theory, and language as a single, unchanging system built on some basic metaphysical precepts. Thus Badawi shifts a bit too easily from the psychology in Coleridge's criticism to terms like *organic form*.[6] It is my contention that Coleridge never satisfactorily adapted a scientific discourse to his literary criticism until 1815, and if he occasionally used critical formulas like *organic form* in the earlier Shakespeare criticism, he did so with far less confidence. Coleridge's early references to organic form are, I suspect, mostly pilferings of Schlegel without much detailed thinking about the implications and linguistic possibilities of the term. Although the phrase *organic form* may appear occasionally in his earlier lectures and notes, it invariably lacks the biological force that it attains in the later years. And a comparison of the 1818 lectures on Shakespeare with the earlier lectures makes this abundantly clear; when Coleridge uses the word *nature* or *natural* in the literary criticism of the middle years, it generally refers to psychological verisimilitude, but in *Biographia Literaria* the connotations of the same word are almost always biological. To claim, then, as many critics have, that Coleridge's psychological criticism and character studies differ little from similar eighteenth-century studies or his own later criticism is an historically inaccurate overstatement produced by an unwillingness to look closely at Coleridge's critical language and to discover all that is peculiarly Coleridge's and specifically dated.

THAT COLERIDGE'S LITERARY CRITICISM between 1800 and 1812 should be so predominantly psychological and so pervasively peppered with psychological terms is of course to be expected, since during this time he devoted a vast amount of time and effort to psychology. No doubt psychology and his contribution to it are central to Coleridge's entire opus, and it is easy to see why scholars like I. A. Richards and Richard Haven claim it is the main pillar of his whole system. Paul Deschamps writes that Coleridge's method is above all else "une sorte de psychanalyse idéaliste. . . . [Elle] a la rigueur de la psychanalyse; comme elle, elle essaie d'atteindre au-delà de la zone claire de la conscience les regions profondes où se cachent les mobiles véritables des actions de l'homme. Mais ce que découvre Coleridge, lorsqu'il pénètre ainsi dans le domaine du subconscient, ce sont des besoins profonds de l'âme, non pas seulement des instincts élémentaires liés aux grandes lois physiologiques, comme le fait le psychanalyse moderne."[7] Yet at other periods of his life, psychology had a more secondary role, and his writings were sometimes far more political or biological than psychological. Only in these middle years, when Coleridge was assimilating the German philosophers and Neoplatonists while working to overthrow Hartley's mechanistic psychology, was psychology the undisputed center of his literary as well as extraliterary work: by 1798 Coleridge had become pretty much disillusioned with politics, the passion of his early years, and by 1800 he had started to devote much of his energy to psychology, 1801 being the rather arbitrary date given for his break with Hartley and the beginning of his own psychological work. He writes Poole in March of this year: "The interval since my last Letter has been filled up by me in the most intense Study. If I do not greatly delude myself, I have not only completely extricated the notions of Time, and Space; but have overthrown the doctrine of Association, as taught by Hartley, and with it all the irreligious metaphysics of modern Infidels—."[8]

Many critics have realized that this apparent break with Hartley is in fact more of a swerve. Without underestimating the difference in Coleridge's and Hartley's respective systems, many critics rightly maintain that Coleridge's psychology naturally carries a great deal of residue from the Hartleyan and associational tradition, a most important point for my argument concerning his psychological vocabulary. Sir Leslie Stephen has noted that even in these years of radical change in his thinking, Coleridge "still sticks to Hartley and the Association doctrine," and James Volant Baker argues that Coleridge's "uneasiness with the general psychology of Locke and Hartley would not be incompatible with the acceptance of the fact of association; Kant accepted it too as a psychological fact."[9] Especially before 1810, Coleridge operates in this associational framework, implementing many important changes yet often following its language and its concepts quite closely. As often with Coleridge, the position between traditional beliefs and his own variations on those beliefs leads Coleridge to think and write about psychology with unusual energy. In defending and promulgating his position, moreover, Coleridge focuses the debate, as he commonly does, on language and definitions of the mind's actions.

Since literature provides for Coleridge the most outstanding case studies and the finest examples of the workings of the mind objectified for observation, the presence of this associational discourse is most readily found in his literary criticism, where the psychological truth of great art could be demonstrated and his psychological model validated. Again it is a mistake to claim that Coleridge's early literary theory has the fully dynamic dimension that it later acquires when he draws on his scientific knowledge. For in these early years his formal criticism is still grounded in a psychology of associations and passions, a good example of which is a report of one of his 1811 lectures. Here Coleridge says, "Domestic feelings themselves of the best and tenderest kind might be borrowed not only from books, but even from the heart, and might be so happily combined by wit as to make a pleasing work—and yet the man not be a poet. . . . That gift of true Imagination, that capability of reducing a multitude into a unity of effect or by strong passion to modify series of thoughts into one predominant thought or feeling—those were faculties which might be cultivated and improved but could not be acquired" (*Shakespearean Criticism*, 2:62–63). Aptly, Coleridge begins here by rejecting an interpretive code, "domestic feeling," which during his political years had been an important touchstone for poetic excellence. When politics become less important, however, the political phrase is usurped in favor of a definition of the imagination made up of primarily associational, psychological terms: *passion, series of thoughts, one predominant thought or feeling*, and *faculties*. Later I will return to some of these terms in order to examine more fully their psychological significance, but even a superficial comparison of this passage with his more famous 1815 definition of the secondary imagination, which "dissolves, diffuses, dissipates" and "is essentially *vital*" suggests that the later scientific language makes an entirely different definition with a very different meaning, in the same way that the psychological language replaces the earlier political rhetoric in the criticism of his middle years.

In addition to his readings in associational psychology and German idealism, however, Coleridge's own experience, his introspective habit, provides him with some of his most profound psychological insights, and these likewise make appearances in Coleridge's criticism. Any good biography of Coleridge clearly reveals that this period in his life was not only rich with scholastic material but sadly rich in personal psychological traumas as well. Occasionally Coleridge's introspective analyses of these experiences also become tools for naturalizing Shakespeare's text; his analysis of Hamlet's "ratiocinative meditativeness" is no doubt the most celebrated case of a critic making a literary character into a mirror image of himself. Although both of the following passages are classic interpretations of Hamlet's problem, their close coincidence with Coleridge's own problems has been remarked by many readers since Coleridge first presented them. In 1813 he writes of Shakespeare:

> In Hamlet I conceive him to have wished to exemplify the moral necessity of a due balance of our attention to outward objects and our meditation on inward thoughts —a due balance between the real and imaginary world. In Hamlet this balance does not exist—his thoughts, images, and fancy [being] far more vivid than his perceptions, and his perceptions instantly passing thro' the medium of his contemplations, and acquiring as they pass a form and color not naturally their own. Hence great, enormous, intellectual activity, and a consequent proportionate aversion to real action, with all its symptoms and accompanying qualities. (*Shakespearean Criticism*, 1:34)

Likewise his discussion of Hamlet in 1811 could be a discussion of his own paralyzing mental habits. Whether Coleridge has "a smack of Hamlet" himself, as he claims,[10] or whether it is Hamlet who has a smack of Coleridge is certainly debatable here:

> Shakespeare wished to impress upon us the truth, that action is the chief end of existence—that no faculties of intellect, however brilliant, can be considered valuable, or indeed otherwise than as misfortunes, if they withdraw us from, or render us repugnant to action, and lead us to think and think of doing, until the time has elapsed when we can do anything effectually. . . . He is a man living in meditation, called upon to act by every motive human and divine, but the great object of his life is defeated by continually resolving to do, but doing nothing but resolve. (2:154–55)

In 1808, moreover, Coleridge again appears in his criticism when he prepares to make a subtle criticism of tragic drama by fashioning a linguistic distinction between remorse and regret, two words that certainly occupied Coleridge's own thinking about himself at this time: "That regret and remorse are feelings different in kind, and not merely as degrees and modifications [of] one and the same feeling, is a fact which it only requires solitude and sincere quiet self-questioning to establish in the mind so that no sophistry can reason it away, no fear of being deemed superstitious and unenlightened by philosophy can scare it, no ridicule scoff it out of conscience." He continues on this digression, referring to his own experiences and those of his friends, and then concludes with an almost paradigmatic example of naturalization, of finding models for literary criticism in the critic's private experiences:

> In cases, I mean to say, not only independent of our will but out of ourselves, we find no difficulty distinguish-

COLERIDGE'S SHAKESPEARE CRITICISM

ing regret from remorse, and in what regards our own selves, yet which is not voluntary, the same distinction, one would think, ought rationally to be made. Yet here commences the difference. We do not, indeed, in the latter more than in the former case confound or lose the distinction; but yet in perhaps a majority of instances, however unconscious of blame we may feel ourselves, yet a something more than regret will mingle with regret; a certain something will haunt and sadden the heart, which if not remorse is, however, a phantom and counterfeit of remorse. May not this be a fact meant to make us sensible that, however independent the calamity may be of any moral fault as its proximate of immediate cause, it may nevertheless, and often will be yet a distant effect of something morally wrong in our past actions; or—for why should I be ashamed of that which tho' reason cannot comprehend, nay even seems to start from, yet of which all nations of the earth in one form or other have prostrated themselves before the mysterious reality—a distant effect of guilt of ages past. (2 : 167–68)

Coleridge's application of this distinction to a particular play has never been found. But the subtle Coleridgean insight of this semantic differentiation indicates that he was preparing to employ it in an equally subtle fashion to the drama he was criticizing. These were times of intense psychological searching and learning for Coleridge, and whether he acquired his information from the academies or his own subterraneous mind he rarely lost an opportunity to use it as a light for his literary criticism. That one often loses sight of the literature while Coleridge digresses on these long psychological disquisitions indicates only that for Coleridge the psychological text is at least as important as the literary one.

ALTHOUGH THE MORE PERSONAL INSTANCES of naturalization are often the most interesting, the use of scholastic psychology, particularly associationism, is the most common language in Coleridge's criticism in these years. I. A. Richards has pointed out that contiguity and similarity are the two most important ideas of the associational psychology that Coleridge was weaned on,[11] and Walter Jackson Bate gives a direct and succinct summary of this trend which so pervasively imbues Coleridge's literary work: "Associationism, in its simplest and most general sense, implies only that ideas which are similar or which have repeatedly occurred simultaneously or in succession tend automatically to evoke one another. Thus, by repeated experience, the perception of a *cause* may lead us to think of or look for an *effect*. By resemblance, moreover, a picture recalls the thought of its original. . . . Or association may work by *contiguity* in time or place: the odor of an apple may suggest the color and shape of it; the idea of a given place may recall the idea of another seen next to it or near it. In addition to cause and effect, resemblance, and contiguity, other less basic principles of mental connection may be cited. That of contrariety would be one."[12] To this outline we should add of course the emotions and feelings, since it is often these that act as the crucial links between different images and ideas. The model may still be too sketchy and fail to do justice to the subtleties that associational theory is capable of. Yet it does provide a rough outline and model of the associational mind that literary critics in the late eighteenth century used to test the veracity and verisimilitude of the characters they read.

In his critical readings of Shakespeare's characters, Coleridge follows his associational model and its language quite closely at times, but regularly adds special meanings and additions to modify it. The foundation for a long and strikingly unliterary analysis of *Romeo and Juliet*, for example, is the idea that "love is not, like hunger, a mere appetite: it is an associative quality" (2:108). Yet, if this analysis is a kind of associational criticism, the terms and meanings are clearly Coleridge's own, not those of his mechanistic contemporaries who sometimes had difficulty distinguishing animal consciousness from human consciousness. Thus early in the lecture he begins his long explanation of the psychology of love by defining his terms precisely:

> I certainly do not mean as a general maxim, to justify so foolish a thing as what goes by the name of love at first sight; but, to express myself more accurately, I should say that there is, and has always existed, a deep emotion of the mind, which might be called love momentaneous—not love at first sight, nor known by the subject of it to be or to have been such, but after many years of experience. . . . I have to defend the existence of love, as a passion in itself fit and appropriate to human action,—I say fit for human nature, and not only so, but peculiar to it, unshared either in degree or kind by our fellow creatures: it is a passion which it is impossible for any creature to feel, but a being endowed with reason, with the moral sense, and with the strong yearnings, which like all other powerful effects in nature, prophesy some future effect. (2:113)

Here the perception of a cause, the emotions of love, leads Coleridge to look for an effect, so that, following Hartley fairly closely, he argues that passionate love generates domestic affections through the power of association and consequently becomes the first step to a more moral society. Coleridge writes that there is something "peculiar to our nature, which answers the moral end," and it manifests it-self in the first awakening of love and affection: "The first feeling that would strike a reflecting mind, wishing to see mankind not only in an amiable but a just light, would be that beautiful feeling in the moral world, the brotherly and sisterly affections,—the existence of strong affection greatly modified by the difference of sex; made more tender, more graceful, more soothing and conciliatory by the cir-cumstances of the difference, yet still remaining perfectly pure, perfectly spiritual" (2:116). Like Hartley, Coleridge says that these affections increase their domain by multiply-ing through contiguity:

> By dividing the sisterly and fraternal affections from the conjugal, we have in truth, two loves, each of them as strong as any affection can be, consistently with the per-formance of our duty, and the love we should bear to our neighbor. Then, by the former preceding the latter, the latter is rendered more pure, more even, and more con-stant: the wife has already the discipline of pure love in the character of the sister. . . . To all this are to be added the beautiful gradations of attachment which distin-guish human nature; from sister to wife, from wife to child. (2:116)

As love grows through association, "the affections become those which urge us to leave the paternal nest. We arrive at a definite time of life, and feel passions that invite us to enter into the world; and this new feeling assuredly coalesces with a new object" (2:117).

After sketching this psychological backdrop (taking up the vast majority of the lecture), Coleridge is finally prepared to comment on *Romeo and Juliet*, the long discussion of psychological terms being, from Coleridge's point of view, absolutely necessary for understanding characters who are so much more complicated than their literary surface would suggest. The connection between this digressive prelude on associational emotions and the play itself, moreover, is logical and smooth for Coleridge. Shakespeare, he claims, knew of psychological maturation through association, and he "looked at the subject of love in this dignified light" (2:118). For Shakespeare,

> the mind of man searches for something which shall add to his perfection—which shall assist him; and he also yearns to lend his aid in completing the moral nature of another. Thoughts like this will occupy many of his serious moments: imagination will accumulate on imagination, until at last some object attracts his attention, and to this object the whole weight and impulse of his feelings will be directed.
>
> Who shall say this is not love? Here is system, but it is founded upon nature: here are associations: here are strong feelings, natural to us as men, and they are directed and finally attached to one object. (2:118)

At the beginning of the play, therefore, Romeo is simply the victim of an aberrant associational mind, impulsively wandering among objects of desire, searching for an ideal object to associate with an ideal mental image: "Romeo tells us what was Shakespeare's purpose: he shows us that he looked at Rosaline with a different feeling from that which he looked at Juliet. Rosaline was the object to which his over-full heart has attached itself in the first instance: our imperfect nature, in proportion as our ideas are vivid, seeks after something in which these ideas may be realized" (2:119). Thus Romeo's capriciousness is an example of a common psychological problem, understood by Coleridge in the terms of an associational vocabulary, and resulting in a reading which, though it may be sound, is unmistakably more psychology than an

Aristotlean literary criticism that adheres closely to the confines of the primary text.

This kind of associational and psychological criticism appears regularly in Coleridge's literary work, although perhaps not so obviously as in *Romeo and Juliet*, where even
Mercutio becomes a kind of psychological case study whose
"whole world was, as it were, subject to his law of association" (2:98). As in the eighteenth century, this kind of
criticism usually appears in character studies, but this psychological vocabulary also accounts for a large amount of
Coleridge's formal criticism, in which "curiosity" and "unity
of interest" figure so prominently. Elinor S. Shaffer has written on Coleridge's character criticism in a fine study of his
Iago; her emphasis on the reverberations and connotations
of the word *motivation* anticipates my linguistic emphasis
here. The material for her argument is mostly taken from
unpublished passages in Coleridge's "Opus Magnum" with
which she attempts to provide a context for some of his
more controversial comments on *Othello*, while her focus is
Coleridge's celebrated remark on Iago's final soliloquy: "The
motive-hunting of motiveless malignity—how awful! In itself fiendish; while yet he was allowed to wear the divine
image, too fiendish for his own steady view." [13] Many readers, Shaffer points out, have misunderstood these comments
and occasionally objected to them loudly, F. R. Leavis being
one of the shriller voices. Yet to understand them fully means
understanding the complex connotations and the special
psychological meaning of the word *motive* for Coleridge, the
first step in this understanding being a distinction between
"Self-love and a Self that loves." For Coleridge, self-love ne-
cessitates an "abandonment to its animal life," since this
kind of love is determined from without by "the law of the
senses and organization"; here "the body becomes our Self,"
a secondary self, and it is dependent on proximity for its
emotions. Genuine love, where the true self acts, on the

other hand, is freely chosen and not tied to material limits. Noting the difference between these two kinds of love accordingly elucidates Coleridge's definition of motive and his analysis of Iago:

> The method of seeking out all of Iago's declared motives and comparing their strengths is, in short, wholly useless as a means of comprehending Iago. The inconsistency of the character, Coleridge has said, is "appropriate"; and in the analysis of the self that we have just reviewed he has shown us the reason why. Iago's is a character thoroughly alienated from its true self, a character whose "secondary self" is directed in fragmentary and unwilled fashion toward the passing things of the world. The true self destroyed, animal sensation and the "heap of perceptions" become dominant. The self casts itself outward . . . onto proximate objects. The sensuality of Iago's character has often been noted, and sometimes felt to be inconsistent with his "rationality." But it is clear from Coleridge's analysis that the two stand in closest possible relationship.[14]

This conception of character and motivation, moreover, explains the peculiarly little time that Coleridge devotes to Othello, since Iago is in fact Othello's "objectified self," and understanding what happens to Othello means first understanding the meaning of Iago. They are complements, and both their last speeches contain the rhetoric of an alienated self still capable of a reminiscence of a true self and subsequently required to delude itself with "motives" and excuses. Likewise, what seems like a quibble—Coleridge's differentiation of Leontes' jealous character and Othello's character, "the true Othello's not jealous character"—is actually a fine discrimination which derives from the same code, Leontes' motives resulting from "a *vice* of the mind, a culpable despicable tendency,"[15] while Othello's motives originally spring from his genuine self and are thus good. We can add to this list Coleridge's comments on the scene in *Hamlet* in which Claudius attempts to pray. Coleridge finds motive-mongering once again the key to the scene, and he notes: "O what a lesson concerning the essential difference between wishing and willing, and the folly of all motive-mongering, while the individual still remains" (*Shakespearean Criticism*, 1:30).

Using loaded terms like *motive* or involved models of associational love, Coleridge naturalizes dramatic characters in this way primarily to suggest the vast psychological complexities that he sees beneath the surface of the plays, and thus to bring the characters more fully to life. "Shakespeare's characters," Coleridge says, "are like those in life, to be *inferred* by the reader, not *told to* him" (1:201). They should have, in short, the psychological mysteries and complications of living men and women; for Coleridge this means they should appear with something like the contradictory nature that Iago has—"fiendish; while yet he was allowed to wear the divine image." Consisting of diverse or opposite elements is a better way of describing this kind of character, and used as a literary code it frequently supplements (and in one sense replaces) the simple associational model. An 1805 notebook entry illustrates how important this way of perceiving men and women is for Coleridge; here he analyzes his own difficulties with man's seemingly contradictory makeup, his own "uneasiness at a non-harmony, the wish not to see any thing admirable where you find, especially in the moral character, any thing low or contemptible, and the consequent wish to avoid the struggle with—this antinomadic feeling, this (what shall I say?) *knowing, feeling,* a man to be *one,* yet not understanding how to think of him but as two."[16] As an example of this problem he names Samuel Richardson, a man who, aptly enough, is as complex as his own fictional characters: according to Coleridge, Richardson is a fine man and writer in many ways, yet he is also "oozy, hypocritical, praise-mad, canting, envious, concupiscent" and "to understand & draw *him* would be to produce [a character] almost equal to any of his own."[17] A large number of Coleridge's character studies proceed along these same lines, where fullness of character means a complexity defined by a kind of contradiction, and the contradiction is very often located—as it is in Iago's character—in a disproportionate ratio of moral honesty and intellectual prowess. Hamlet, "with all the strength of motive," cannot act for vague metaphysical reasons; Richard III has "pride of intellect, without moral feeling"; and Bolingbroke, who closely resembles Richard, differs only in the way his character manifests itself: "In Richard III. the pride of intellect makes use of ambition as its means; in Bolingbroke the gratification of ambition is the end, and talents are the means" (*Shakespearean Criticism*, 2:141).

Besides showing Coleridge's partial debt to the associational model, describing Coleridge's psychology of character in this fashion avoids, I believe, a common tendency to see Coleridge as part psychological critic and part moral critic, concerned on the one hand with psychological accuracy and on the other with philosophical truth.[18] (This was the spurious dichotomy that associational psychologists tended to perpetuate.) Actually human psychology is a ratio or interaction of intellect and morality. The one does not belong to the realm of psychology and the other to the realm of metaphysics: the tension between the two, rather, is what accounts for psychological completeness in both real persons and fictional characters. For Coleridge, psychological verisimilitude is, as it was with the eighteenth-century associational critics, a most important feature in Shakespeare's drama, but he develops a new psychological vocabulary or model to designate that verisimilitude, a vocabulary that includes morality and "the heart."

As THE ANALYSIS OF ROMEO'S LOVE SUGGESTS, passions are important psychological facts in Coleridge's revised model of the mind. The significance and importance of the word *passion*, however, appears even greater when it becomes obvious how much Coleridge's theory of dramatic unity has in common with the eighteenth-century notion of ruling passion. Quite frequently, that is, Coleridge analyzes passions and their role in a play, and these analyses invariably pinpoint the meaning of that play. The meaning of *Othello* lies partly in "Iago's passionless character, all *will* in intellect" but mostly in the growth of Othello's destructive passion. The heart of *Richard II* is Richard's incontinent passionate character, his "constant overflow of feelings, incapability of controlling them; waste of that energy that should be received for action in the passion and effort of resolves and menaces, and consequent exhaustion" (*Shakespearean Criticism*, 1:139–40). And it is not Edgar's intellectual character but Lear's smoldering passion that is the central force in *King Lear*: "In Edgar's ravings Shakespeare all the while lets you see a fixed purpose, a practical end in view,—in Lear's, there is only the brooding of one anguish, an eddy without progression" (1:58). Again this kind of criticism springs from eighteenth-century practices, yet as Coleridge modifies and reworks his thinking on psychology so that passions involved not only emotions but emotions in relation to thoughts, this particular critical terminology changes significantly, paving the way for Coleridge's more complex theory of dramatic form. With *passion* as a pivotal term, Coleridge redirects his psychological vocabulary and thus his literary criticism from character analysis to analysis of dramatic form: just as the character is the center of Shakespeare's plays, so this character's mind provides the key to the play's form; for Coleridge the connection between the two is made clear only by highlighting and defining a number of crucial psychological terms and ideas such as passion, dream, and curiosity.

Coleridge's unfinished essay "On the Passions" is doubtless the best evidence of the special and complicated connotations of this term for Coleridge, and it consequently illuminates much of his dramatic criticism. The "primary sense of the word," he writes, derives

> from pati} {-agere, to undergo} {-to act upon. Passion, a state of undergoing. . . . By the passions generally, and described therefore by their generic or common characters, we mean—a state of emotion, which tho' it may have its predisposing cause in the Body, and its occasion in external Incidents or Appearances, is yet not *immediately* produced by the incidents themselves, but by the person's Thoughts and reflections concerning them. Or more briefly: A Passion is a state of emotion which, having its immediate cause not in Things, but in our Thoughts of Things—or—A Passion is a state of emotion which, whatever its object or occasion may be, in ourselves or out of ourselves, has its proper and immediate cause not in this, but in our Thoughts respecting it.[19]

In short, a particular interaction of thoughts and incidents determine a particular passion. And passion, in describing the place where thoughts, objects, and feelings unite, becomes an invaluable key when applied to drama, for it allows Coleridge to describe as one both a play's particular meaning and the agent that unifies the separate incidents and elements in a play.

An excellent example of this word at work is his criticism of *The Winter's Tale*. Maintaining at the beginning of his lecture "that Shakespeare ought not to be judged in detail, but on the whole," Coleridge continues with a favorite maxim and then describes the units of various episodes at the beginning of the play through the movement of its central passion:

> A pedant differed from his master in cramping himself with certain established rules. Whereas the master regarded rules as always controllable by the subservient to the end. The passion to be delineated in *The Winter's Tale* was *jealousy*. Shakespeare's description of this, however, was perfectly philosophical: the mind, in its first harbouring of it, became mean and despicable, and the first sensation was perfect shame, arising from the consideration of having possessed an object unworthily, of degrading a person to a thing. The mind that once indulges this passion has a predisposition, a vicious weakness, by which it kindles a fire from every spark, and from circumstances the most innocent and indifferent finds fuel to feed the flame. (*Shakespearean Criticism*, 2:227)

What modifies and synthesizes thoughts and events in the mind is a passion; likewise what synthesizes diverse events and ideas in a Shakespearean play is a dominant passion—in this case jealousy—apprehended and presented by the imagination. "That blending of thoughts in each other," Coleridge says in 1811, "or, rather into one passion, . . . was one of the greatest criterions of a true poet,—which implied three constituent parts, namely, sensibility, imagination and the powers of association" (2:65). In the poet, this union of thoughts in passion can be perceived as the synthesis of intellectual judgment and emotional genius (the latter being the randomness for which Shakespeare was both praised and condemned in the eighteenth century). In a play like *The Winter's Tale* a central passion creates the emotional coherency that binds the separate incidents. Moreover, just as a passionate will in an individual ultimately has more truth-content than mere intellectual motivation, the ruling passion in a play is more important than the intellectual arrangement of a play.

Although the well-known psychological tradition of this concept of ruling passion makes Coleridge's use rather imitative in some ways, his extrapolations from and modifications of that tradition are what account for some of his most brilliant observations. His addition of thought and judgment to passion's power is one of these modifications, and his ability to apply the same index consistently to characters like the passionless Iago indicates its range. Further, when Coleridge uses this index, in a modified, more psychologically complex manner, to discuss audience response, it allows him to describe dramatic unity in a far more interesting way than was usual. Coleridge faces the same psychological question here that he did when he posed the problem in terms of the artist: how is the perception of discrete sensations and separate ideas unified into a single experience? And once again, his notions of how passions function in the mind provide the solution to the question, although, in doing so, this psychology of passions now suggests an important connection between Coleridge's theory of dramatic unity and his pleasure principle. The associational vocabulary is still very much present: words like *sensations*, *corresponding ideas*, *impress*, and *mental excitement*. But when the predominant passion is seen in terms of the audience

NATURALIZATION AND PSYCHOLOGY

there are some important changes: first, the passionate imagination's role as a unifying agent in a play is revamped so that it now becomes a kind of mental stimulant which elicits a "unity of interest"; second, to maintain a special consistency in his literary criticism and concomitantly to do justice to the complications of art, Coleridge introduces a unique interpretive model based on his psychology of dreams and passion's part in dreams.

Some of his own poetry being so dreamlike, it is certainly not surprising that Coleridge thought much and carefully about the psychological subtleties of dreaming and their relation to the artistic experience of the audience. He makes this connection between art and dreaming most lucidly in an 1804 notebook entry, when he says poetry is a "rationalized dream, dealing to manifold Forms our own Feelings, that never perhaps were attached by us consciously to our own personal Selves.—What is *Lear*, the *Othello*, but a divine Dream. . . ."[20] And later he observes in *The Friend*:

> I have long wished to devote an entire work to the subject of Dreams, Visions, Ghosts, Witchcraft, &c., in which I might first give, and then endeavor to explain the most interesting and best-attested fact of each, which has come within my knowledge, either from books or personal testimony. I might then explain in a more satisfactory way the mode in which our thoughts in states of morbid slumber, become at times perfectly dramatic (for in certain sorts of dreams the dullest Wight becomes a Shakespeare) and by what law the *Form* of the vision appears to talk to us in its own thoughts in a voice as audible as the shape is visible; and this too oftentimes in connected trains. . . .[21]

Similarly he writes about the intermediate state of dramatic illusion in terms of its dreamy qualities:

In what this consists I cannot better explain than by referring you to the highest degree of it; namely, dreaming. It is laxly said that during sleep, we take our dreams
for realities, but this is irreconcilable with the nature of
sleep, which consists in a suspension of the voluntary
and, therefore, of the comparative power. The fact is
that we pass no judgement either way: we simply do not
judge them to be unreal, in consequence of which the
images act on our minds, as far as they act at all by their
own force as images.

Doubtless there is a difference between a dream and an art
work, but Coleridge insists that the difference is "in the
degree rather than in the kind" (*Shakespearean Criticism*,
1:116).

The use of the Hobbesian term *trains* in the passage from
The Friend indicates that Coleridge still has one foot firmly
on associational thinking when he discusses dreams, but
this does not mean, as some critics maintain,[22] that he views
dreaming as a passive state. Humphry House has convincingly demonstrated that for Coleridge feelings, emotions,
and passions are active powers that unify and vitalize associated images.[23] And, at a number of points in his essay "On
the Passions" Coleridge himself identifies passion with action, thus setting up a psychological foundation for a round-
about Aristotelean conception of drama, since these passions
operate much the same for the dreamer and the artist. In two
different notebook entries of 1804, Coleridge remarks how
"all Passion unifies as it were by natural Fusion"[24] and how
in dreams diverse forms are connected "in a state of fusion
with some Feeling or other, that is the distorted Reflection
of my Day-Feelings."[25] In sleep the imagination becomes the
appendage of the passion, as he explains elsewhere, and
the passion becomes the "seat of manifestation a shechinah
in the heart . . . an animant self-conscious pendulum."[26]

Dreams then are fully alive with an emotional action, and great poets, who are the greatest of dreamers, approximate this union of dynamic feeling and form. Coleridge in other words believes passion and feeling have more to do with the imagination and the energy of the irrational than with simple sensuous response, so that in dreaming and in art these become active forces and agents of the imagination.

Coleridge thus opposes critics like Joseph Priestley, maintaining that in great art the vehicle of true passion is an active dream-state, a moving atmosphere, not static sensual particulars. Hence a poem or a play is most beautiful and most impassioned when it appears most like a flowing dream—"the dreamlike continuity" of Richardson's *Clarissa* serves as an example, as does *The Faerie Queene*, where there is "marvelous independence and true imaginative absence of all particular space or time. . . . It is the domain neither of history or geography; it is ignorant of all artificial boundary, all material obstacles; it is truly in (and of) Faery, that is, of mental space. The poet has placed you in a dream, a chained sleep, and you neither wish nor have the power, to inquire where you are, or how you got there."[27] Passion and thought, which were separate heuristic touchstones in Coleridge's poetics in the 1790s, are now one, through his analysis of dreams: thought and feeling are now united in a dream code whose center is an active feeling. Aptly, one of Coleridge's favorite poets of the 1790s is now ousted: "A Poet's *Heart* & *Intellect* should be combined, *intimately* combined & *unified*, with the great appearances in Nature—& not merely held in solution and loose mixture with them. . . . The truth is—Bowles has indeed the *sensibility* of a poet; but he has not the *Passion* of a great Poet."[28] Shakespeare, however, always survives, and, following Schlegel, Coleridge points out that *Romeo and Juliet* creates a dreamy illusion where a "*unity of feeling* pervades the whole. . . .

All is youth and spring. . . . The same feeling commences, goes through, and ends the play" (*Shakespearean Criticism*, 2:124). Like Spenser, Shakespeare appeals to faculties "which have no relation to time and place," and the passionate dream that he creates is truly "the poet's power."

This perception of drama as a kind of dream provides, needless to say, the basis of Coleridge's more famous statements about the special kind of illusion that art creates, and moreover accounts for the unity of interest which Shakespeare's plays so beautifully elicit. For Coleridge, dramatic illusion is like a dream, part passive but also quite active; it is the psychological state of "Psychosomatic Ology" where "feelings emerging in consciousness on the fringes of awareness are physiological as well as psychological happenings."[29] Using this active-passive model in an 1805 lecture on stage illusion, Coleridge accordingly begins his discussion with a description of a person's consciousness during a nightmare, partially awake, partially asleep, partially active, partially passive. Although he hedges in the first sentence, dreams again become the telling underpinning for the interpretation of art:

> The nightmare is not a mere dream, but takes place when the waking state of the brain is re-commencing, and most often during a rapid alternation, a *twinkling*, as it were, of sleeping and waking. . . . The mind . . . which at all times, with and without our distinct consciousness, seeks for and assumes some outward cause for every impression from without, and which in sleep by aid of the imaginative faculty converts its judgements respecting the cause into a present image, as being the cause,—the mind, I say, in this case deceived by past experience, attributes the painful sensation received to a correspondent agent—an assassin, for in-

stance, stabbing at the side, or a goblin sitting on the
breast, . . . and thus we unite the actual perceptions, or
their immediate reliques, with the phantoms of the inward sense, and thus so confound the half-waking, half-
sleeping, reasoning power, that we actually do pass a
positive judgement for the reality of what we see and
hear, tho' often accompanied by doubt and self-questioning. (*Shakespearean Criticism*, 1:179–80)

Both dreams and stage illusion absorb the viewer into
their feeling and form, and subsequently, both elicit an interest in each part which is equal to the interest in the whole.
This unity of interest thus accounts for the particular logic
of a play as the audience perceives it. Obviously this code is
Coleridge's replacement for the classical three unities that
he rejected early in his career in favor of "homogeneity, pro-
portionateness, and totality of interest" (1:4). And the main
reason for this change is that the classical unities imparted a
kind of verisimilitude to drama that Coleridge disallowed,
while unity of interest implied a reality that was not so an-
noyingly factual but rather more fluidly and idealistically
dreamlike. In his 1811–12 lectures he proposes "unity of interest" as a literary code, and notes "that the unities of time
and place were not essential to drama, and that to suppose
them necessary was to suppose as evident a falsehood as that
the drama impresses with pleasure only as it is supposed to
be reality" (2:55). And discussing *Hamlet*, he argues that in
"any direct form to have kept Hamlet's love for Ophelia before the audience, would have made a breach in the unity of
interest," since incidental and quotidian facts must always
be subservient to the controlling passion that lifts a play
above the mundane (1:28). Similarly he faults a number of
contemporary poems for failing to maintain this unity of interest. Poems like *The Pleasures of Tea-drinking, The Plea-*

sures of Wine-drinking, The Pleasures of Hope, and *The Pleasures of Fear*

> were mere abstract ideas, and which poems were made up by heaping together a certain number of images and a certain number of thoughts, and then merely tying [them] together with a string as if it had [been] bought at a penny the yard. What was the consequence? When the artist had come to the end of one thought, another must arise with which there was not the least connection of mind, or even of logic (which was the least connection of a poet), or of passions, frequently acting by contrast, but always justifying themselves—no, there was no such connection, but a full pause ensues and the reader must begin again. (2:73–74)

Intricately bound up with this theory of aesthetic interest and thus with his psychology of dreams and passions are Coleridge's ideas about the pleasure of art. Poetry, Coleridge says, "is the art of communicating whatever we wish to communicate, so as to both express and produce excitement, . . . for the purpose of immediate pleasure" (2:41). One of its essential requirements is that it be *"impassionate,* since images must be vivid, in order to move our passions and awaken our affections" (2:212). Aesthetic passions, in short, elicit a response from the audience, which is a kind of interest, an awakening of feeling or affection, and this interest is at once a pleasurable excitement and a fundamental step in the communication of poetry's truth. Passion and excitement are correlatives, as Coleridge indicates in some notes on "Venus and Adonis" (1:193); passions in a poem evoke an emotional response through the audience's sympathy, a response that can be characterized as mental excitement. "The very assumption that we are reading the work of a poet supposes that he is in a continuous state of excitement" (2:42), and the interaction of the work's feeling with the audience's feeling Coleridge associates with the pleasurable excitement that a play creates in a viewer's mind.

Doubtless this notion of emotional excitement has something in common with Hartley's theory of mental vibrations. But Coleridge makes certain to distinguish it and place his excitement in the realm of the imagination, the realm of dreams and illusion: "All may be delighted that Shakespeare did not anticipate, and write his plays with any conception of that strong excitement of the senses, that inward endeavor to make every thing appear reality which is deemed excellent as to the effort of the present day" (2:57). Further, he writes in some notes on *The Tempest*, "The principle and only genuine excitement ought to come from within,—from the moved and sympathetic imagination; whereas, where so much is addressed to the mere external senses of seeing and hearing, the spiritual vision is apt to languish, and the attraction from without will withdraw the mind from the proper and only legitimate interest which is intended to spring from within" (1:118). Hence, when Coleridge calls Prospero's speeches in the second scene "the finest examples of retrospective narration for the purpose of exciting immediate interest," the pleasurable excitement and subsequent interest he refers to are neatly related in an aesthetic of dreams and passions. The pleasure is different from that described by materialistic psychology; dreamlike, it is "something nobler, for which we have not a name, but distinct altogether from what in ordinary language of common sense can be brought under the name of pleasure" (2:49). Clearly dependent on his own special model of the mind, Coleridge's aesthetic interest and pleasure appeal, therefore, to a faculty that is neither entirely sensually interested, like Burke's aesthetic of the sublime, nor entirely without passionate interest, like Kant's. Rather Coleridge's aesthetic pleasure and interest inhabit a middle state which is very much like a passionate dream, where the strength of the ruling emotion summons the mind to attention, and the suspension of disbelief represents an imaginative and absolute concentration on the spectacle.[30]

WORKING IN CONJUNCTION with the understanding and the imagination, an art work can create the excitement and interest that Coleridge associates with a dream in two ways. One way is by imparting a dream-world strangeness to ordinary objects and events, as Coleridge himself does in "The Rime of the Ancient Mariner" and which he describes in his essay "On Poesy and Art." "Whilst it recalls the sights and sounds that had accompanied the occasions of the original passions, poetry impregnates them with an interest not their own by means of the passions, and yet tempers the passion by the calming power which all distinct images exert on the human soul."[31] A second and more complex way, though, is through the formal movement of a work of literature in which unity of interest is produced by a dynamic interaction of the different parts of an art work, or, more specifically, through the interaction of the similarities and contrasts in that work. Describing his experience of a picturesque scene in 1804, Coleridge comments on this kind of perception when he observes that, along with the imaginative wholeness of the scene, there "must be added the Lights & Shades, sometimes *sunshiny*, sometimes *snowy*: sometimes shade-coloured, sometimes dingy—whatever distance, air tints, reflected Light, and the feeling connected with *the* Object (for all Passion unifies as it were by natural Fusion) have in bringing out, in melting down differences and contrast, according as the mind finds it necessary to the completion of the idea of Beauty."[32]

In the same way, moreover, a Shakespearean play can be analyzed in terms of the contrasts and similarities that a guiding passion brings into conjunction. In 1804 Coleridge calls this imaginative coupling "the disjunctive conjunctive of the sudden Images *seized* on from external Contingents by Passion and Imagination," differentiating it from the more mechanical "conjunctive disjunctive" of wits.[33] And later he hails the picturesque art of Shakespeare for producing a pleasurable whole "by the balance, counteractions, and inter-modifications, and final harmony of differents."[34] Hence the second way an art work creates interest and pleasure may be seen in terms of a psychology of audience response which is based on the diachronic interaction of the separate parts of the work and in which this interaction becomes the man-ifestation of the emotion followed through each of those parts as a ruling passion. As in a dream, the flowing together of the different images and scenes brings the feeling to life, "admitting a pleasure from the whole, consistent with the consciousness of pleasurable excitement from the compo-nent parts" (*Shakespearean Criticism*, 2:51).

The psychological roots of this dream logic which a poem or play approximates are indeed significant, since they eluci-date some interesting remarks Coleridge makes about the reader's "curiosity," and they furthermore provide a sounder, more sophisticated context for his concern with the first scenes of Shakespeare's plays, the point where interest is first aroused and the formal dream-work initiated. Cole-ridge's comments on the pleasure of poetic meter, for in-stance, spring directly from this psychology of formal inter-est and curiosity. Aptly, the intoxicated atmosphere that meter creates reminds one of a dream: "As far as meter acts in and for itself, it tends to increase the vivacity and suscep-tibility both of the general feelings and the attention. This effect it produces by the continued excitement of surprise, and by quick reciprocations of curiosity still gratified and still re-excited, *which are too slight indeed* to be at any *one moment objects of distinct consciousness,* yet become considerable in their aggregate influence. As a medicated atmosphere, or as wine during animated conversation; they act powerfully, though themselves unnoticed."[35] Similarly, a 1708 review of *The Mysteries of Udolpho* explains how formal contrasts and gradations are necessary for the reader's emotional involvement and curiosity. As with meter, there must be a dynamic interaction of the parts and a "gratification of the Love of Variety with the grat. of the Love of Uniformity."[36] Coleridge writes:

> Four volumes cannot depend entirely on terrific incidents and intricacy of story. They require character, unity of design, a delineation of scenes of real life, and the variety of well supported contrast. The Mysteries of Udolpho are indeed relieved by much elegant description and picturesque scenery; but in the descriptions there is too much of sameness: the pine and the larch tree wave, and the full moon pours its lustre through almost every chapter. Curiosity is raised oftener than it is gratified; or rather, it is raised so high that no adequate gratification can be given; the interest is completely dissolved when once the adventure is finished, and the reader, when he has got to the end of the work, looks about in vain for the spell which has bound him so strongly to it.[37]

For Coleridge, a Gothic romance is of course a different experience from that of a play or a poem, yet his codes for criticizing all three genres have much in common in this passage. Requiring the interaction of similitude and dissimilitude, he criticizes "sameness." This "sameness" is equated with unimaginative verisimilitude, and the result is a lack of interest since curiosity and excitement are not abetted. As in a dream, the reader must become a "curious" participant in the twist and turns of a literary drama where the formal progressions are emotional progressions that gratify, frustrate, surprise, and create expectations in the reader-participant: "In dreams one is much less, in the most tranquil dreams, a spectator only—one seems always about to do, or suffering or thinking, or talking."[38]

Whereas *The Mysteries of Udolpho* fails to produce this active curiosity and participation, *The Tempest*, which Coleridge also calls a romance, succeeds beautifully; with each scene Shakespeare shows "admirable judgment and excellent preparation" in creating the linear continuity and contrasts in this play (*Shakespearean Criticism*, 2:137). The juxtaposition of Ariel's and Caliban's entrances is one example of this kind of preparation and development. Another occurs early in the play:

> In reference to preparation, it will be observed that the storm, and all that precedes the tale, as well as the tale itself, serve to develope completely the main character of the drama, as well as the design of Prospero. The manner in which the heroine is charmed asleep fits us for what follows, goes beyond our ordinary belief, and gradually leads us to the appearance and disclosure of a being of the most fanciful and delicate texture, like Prospero, preternaturally gifted.
>
> In this way the entrance of Ariel, if not absolutely forethought by the reader, was foreshewn by the writer. (2:135)

In the same manner, Coleridge comments on the scene in which Prospero puts his daughter to sleep in order to recount his story: "Prospero having cast a sleep upon his daughter, by that sleep stops the narrative at the very moment when it was necessary to break it off, in order *to excite curiosity*, and yet to give the memory and understanding sufficient to carry on the progress of the history uninterruptedly" (2:133, my emphasis). Again, this kind of curiosity and excitement is directly related to Coleridge's concept of stage illusion as a kind of dream; he himself makes this point when he explains how these scenes work through a "poetic faith," a "feeling," and a psychological preparation that closely resembles the mental abandonment to dreams. "Here, what is called poetic faith is required and created, and our common notions of philosophy give way before it: this feeling may be said to be much stronger than historic faith, since for the exercise of poetic faith the mind is previously prepared" (2:135).

The psychological preparation and excitement that Coleridge requires here needs, however, a finer distinction, a distinction that turns on the difference between the two words *surprise* and *expectation*. Listing the first characteristic of Shakespeare's genius, Coleridge accordingly notes the superiority of "expectation in preference to surprise. . . . As the feeling with which we startle at a shooting star, compared with that of watching the sunrise at the pre-established moment, such and so low is surprise compared with expectation" (1:199). Indeed Coleridge may not be entirely consistent with the use of the words themselves, but the semantic distinction is usually implied. In his sixth lecture of 1811, he discusses the difference between wit and fancy in terms of two types of formal interest that clearly translate as surprise and expectation: "There is a wide difference between the talent which gives a sort of electric surprise by a mere turn of a phrase, and that higher ability which produces surprise by a permanent medium, and always leaves something behind it, which satisfies the mind as well as tickles the hearing" (2:91). Further, in his reviews Coleridge consistently disparages the Gothic romances for using surprise, an audience strategy that relies on sensual curiosity rather than imaginative expectation; in *The Monk* and *The Mysteries of Udolpho* "curiosity is a kind of appetite, and hurries headlong on, impatient for its complete gratification."[39] Thus, though he finds much art in *The Mysteries of Udolpho*, his praise is always tepid, primarily because the kind of interest it provokes is either flat or bombastic: "In this contest of curiosity on one side and invention on the other, Mrs. Radcliffe has certainly the advantage. . . . This method is, however, liable to the following inconvenience, that in the search of what is new, an author is apt to forget what is natural. . . . The trite and the extravagant are the Scylla and Charybdis of writers who deal in fiction."[40] Modern novels of this kind rely on sensual curiosity or surprise. Only the reader's most basic impulses are engaged, not his whole psychological makeup; thus he does not wholly participate, as one does in the imaginative world of a dream. Such is "the common modern novel, in which there is no imagination, but a miserable struggle to excite and gratify. . . . Novel-reading of this sort is especially injurious to the growth of the imagination, the judgment, and the morals . . . because it excites mere feelings without at the same time ministering an impulse to action."[41] Later in *Biographia Literaria* he would continue to condemn surprise in art and rail against Cowley's "rhetorical caprices . . . the native product neither of the fancy nor of the imagination; that their operation consists in the excitement of surprise by the juxtaposition and *apparent* reconciliation of widely different or incompatible things. As when for instance, the hills are made to reflect the image of a *voice*" in the lines

> Begin, begin thy noble choice,
> And let the hills around reflect the image of thy
>   voice.[42]

Shakespeare's plays, on the other hand, are masterpieces in the art of creating a formal design through the audience's imaginative curiosity and expectations. Coleridge's description of stage illusion as a kind of dreaming continues to be the foundation for this judgment, although this time he uses the difference in the degree of the two states to illustrate Shakespeare's precise control over the audience's participation in his dream. Coleridge notes that "in sleep we pass at once by sudden collapse into this suspension of will and the comparative power: whereas in an interesting play, read or represented, we are brought up to this point, as far as it is requisite or desirable, gradually, by the art of the poet and the actors, and with the consent and positive aidance of our own will we *choose* to be deceived" (*Shakespearean Criticism*, 1:116). Coleridge continues with perhaps his most direct statement on the dramatic excitement that is inextricably bound to imaginative development, expectation, and the unity of interest: proper illusion, he argues

> depends on the degree of excitement in which the mind is supposed to be. Many things would be intolerable in the first scene of a play that would not at all interrupt our enjoyment in the height of the interest. The narrow cockpit may hold
>
> > The vasty fields of France, or we may cram
> > Within its wooden O the very casques
> > That did affright the air in Agincourt.
>
> And again, on the other hand, many obvious improbabilities will be endured as belonging to the groundwork of the story rather than to the drama, in the first scenes, which would disturb or disentrance us from all illusion in the acme of our excitement, as, for instance, Lear's division of his realm and banishment of Cordelia. But besides this dramatic probability, all the other excel-

117

lences of the drama, as unity of interest . . . and the
charm of language and sentiment for their own sakes,
yet still as far as they tend to increase the inward excitement, and are all means to this chief end, that of producing and supporting this willing illusion. (1:116–17)

As this last passage indicates, Coleridge's interest in the
first scenes of Shakespeare's plays is therefore not so typically Romantic as is usually supposed; that is, Coleridge
does not concentrate on the first scenes because, like many
Romantic critics, he is unable to deal with dramatic development. Rather, precisely because he has a sense of a dramatic
development which springs from the imaginative interest
and expectations provoked by the first scene of a play Coleridge can and does use those first scenes as the hubs of his
criticism. "Shakespeare shewed great judgment in his first
scenes," Coleridge says; "they contained the germ of the ruling passion which was to be developed hereafter" (2:30).
What this means, as I have argued, is quite complex and sophisticated: it connotes a particular psychology of form,
however elusive and idiosyncratic, conceived in terms of audience response and very much dependent on Coleridge's
model of the mind and the vocabulary of that model. Hence
it is not capriciousness or laziness that causes Coleridge to
devote so much time and space to a detailed analysis of the
first scenes in Shakespeare's plays. As with Romeo's seemingly whimsical love, the first scenes in *Hamlet*, *The Tempest*, and *King Lear* are for Coleridge the sparks which light
the reader's curiosity and interest for the entire play. What
he says about *Richard II* is therefore exemplary of much of
his formal criticism during these years: "The judgement
with which Shakespeare always in his first scenes prepares,
and yet how naturally and with what concealment of art, for
the catastrophe. How he presents the *germ* of all the after
events, in Richard's insincerity, pariality, arbitrariness, favor-

itism, and in the proud tempestuous temperament of his barons" (1:138).

The full significance of Coleridge's analyses of these first scenes lies, then, in his subtle though scattered psychology and in the psychological connections between terms like interest, passion, and dreams. That Coleridge proceeds with these connections in mind but never fully explains the psychological foundation on which they are based is unfortunate and sometimes confusing, yet it should not distract us from their enduring critical value. The perceptive richness of his comments on Shakespeare's characters and the first scenes of the plays, his use of curiosity, interest, and pleasure in his drama criticism, and his rethinking of the notion of ruling passion and its relation to dreams, illusion, and the dynamics of art are indications of the sophistication and complexity of Coleridge's psychological poetics and the deep resonances of his psychological vocabulary.[43]

Perhaps more than any other critic in his age, Coleridge trusts his reflection on his own experiences and his own mind as touchstones for his appreciation and understanding of literature. He, more than anyone else, reveals himself in his criticism. Yet his presence there is not what is most impressive; any hack can naturalize literature. Where Coleridge excels is in the knowledge of the mind, his own mind often, which he brings to his reading of literature and uses there as precise and productive tools for literary criticism. Whether it is Hamlet or Coleridge we are reading about in Coleridge's notes seems much less important than that there is a fascinating coincidence of the two, that Coleridge's model of the mind makes characters like Hamlet seem a bit like every reader, and that Coleridge can find in his own mind patterns that make him too a bit like every reader. If many critics naturalize characters and other dimensions of literature so that they come alive in terms of the critic's own mind and psychological models, a good critic like Coleridge first makes his own mind and psychology expansive and penetrating enough to give those readings a breadth and authenticity that can touch many other reader's lives as well. For Coleridge, the psychology that permeated the literary criticism of England in 1800 lacked this authenticity and certainly did not adequately explain his own mind. And his attempt to rectify this situation was an attempt to introduce a revamped psychological language into literary criticism, a language with meanings perhaps too much out of their time. The boldness with which Coleridge sets about this task, his stubborn naturalizations of literary works—these indeed result in some peculiar and occasionally outlandish remarks. The same boldness, however, has given us readings that rank with the best and most provocative of Shakespeare criticism.

CHAPTER FOUR

The *Biographia Literaria* and the Language of Science

*As far as words go, I have become a
formidable chemist.*
COLERIDGE,
to Humphry Davy

WHEN COLERIDGE BEGAN DICTATING his *Biographia Literaria* in 1815, he was at the same time becoming actively involved in a medico-philosophical controversy that was then drawing the attention of most medical men and philosophers in England. The fundamental issue behind the quarrel, a mechanistic versus a dynamic theory of nature, was one Coleridge had argued in one form or another throughout his career. Yet the challenge of modern science specifically had never been so strong nor had it so vociferously demanded his attention as it did in the years from 1814 to 1819. Coleridge's response is well documented: the revised and enlarged version of *The Friend*, his two *Lay Sermons*, the "Hints towards a More Comprehensive Theory of Life," and a series of philosophical letters written between November 1816, and January 1818 all testify to Coleridge's growing concern with the challenge of science and his need to validate his philosophical beliefs with scientific evidence. In one of his letters to C. A. Tulk, Coleridge prefaces a long account of the forces of nature with these remarks: "In my literary Life you will find a sketch of the *subjective* Pole of the Dynamic Philosophy. . . . In the third volume of the Friend, now in the Press, you will find the great *results* of this Philosophy in its relation to Ethics and Theology— while the enclosed Scrawl contains a very, very rude and fragmentary delineation of the *Objective* Pole, or the Science of the Construction of *Nature*."[1] The enclosed scrawl is in fact an abstract of Coleridge's "Theory of Life," his most detailed and comprehensive scientific treatise and a work which refers explicitly to John Abernathy and other major figures in the current medical controversy. The literary life is of course the *Biographia Literaria*, roughly contemporaneous with the "Theory of Life" and likewise in the orbit of the scientific debates. That the *Biographia Literaria* also refers to scientists involved in the medical debate is only tangentially significant, that the *Biographia Literaria* employs much of the scientific language used in the "Theory of Life" and implicitly derives many of its critical models from the scientific models sketched in that work is, however, extremely significant, for it shows Coleridge transferring the scientific discourse which suffused his intellectual life at the time to another discourse, literary criticism. Probably no other alteration in the language of literary criticism has affected practical criticism more.

Coleridge's prolific response to the medical controversy surrounding the composition of the *Biographia Literaria* was, of course, the product of many years of reading and thinking about science. Since his early years at Christ's Hospital, Coleridge flirted on and off with biology and chemistry, and his meeting in 1799 with Humphry Davy marked the beginning of a friendship that inspired Coleridge to seek metaphors for his poetry and solutions to metaphysical problems in scientific research. In one of the rare articles on Coleridge and science, Kathleen Coburn relates how, at its outset, this friendship between the father of the new chemistry and the father of the new criticism was mutually productive: Coleridge shared much of Davy's scientific reading, and as Coleridge searched for the laws within the impalpable, within poems, Davy "was searching out laws of substances hitherto unknown by revealing that beneath the static appearance of the stone, or of the powder . . . there may be the flame, the loud bang, the explosive energy. They were both enraptured by the revelation of unsuspected relationships in the vast diversity of things, inanimate as well as animate." It is not surprising, then, that Coleridge's and Davy's description of the poet and the scientist respectively are strikingly similar or that "Coleridge's description in *Biographia Literaria* of the imagination derives at least some of its vitality and power from the fact that although he is talking about the nature of poetry, he might in places equally be talking about Davy's chemistry."[2]

It is important to realize, however, that these affinities between Coleridge and Davy are based on Davy's work around 1802, ten years before the waning of their intellectual friendship. Coleridge avidly followed Davy's 1802 lectures and read his work for many years after, but the famous marginal note to Boehme's *Aurora* summarizes the vicissitudes of a relationship strained by the demands of modern science:

> O how gladly would I resign my life . . . to procure for mankind such health and longevity to H. Davy, as should enable him to discover the Element of metals, of Sulphur and of Carbon. Oh! he will do it! Yea and may perhaps reveal the synthetic Idea of the Antithets, Attraction and Repulsion.
>
> S. T. C.
>
> Alas! since I wrote the preceding note H. Davy is become Sir Humphry Davy and an Atomist![3]

As M. H. Abrams illustrates in *The Mirror and the Lamp*, the personal misunderstandings between Davy and Coleridge were in part the product of a general rift between science and poetry in the first quarter of the nineteenth century, Coleridge belonging to the poetic school of spirit and imagination and Davy often tending toward a progressive science which was becoming increasingly mechanistic and materialistic. Davy in fact never totally accepted the theories of atomists like Dalton, and he and Coleridge would always remain distant admirers. Yet the gap that atomistic science was creating between poetry and science made it increasingly difficult for them to share and discuss philosophies. Unhappily for the poets, the disparity between the two disciplines could only diminish poetry's value, as scientists claimed that the poetic vision was a fantastic way of knowing with little relevance to the scientific laws of nature. For Coleridge, this claim—that there was an inherent and inescapable conflict between science and poetry—was intolerable, for if the scientific validity of imaginative perception could not be maintained, the moral principles founded on that imaginative perception would be in danger of dissipating as ethereal musings. Thus in the *Treatise on Method* he bemoans a world suffering "from a subversion of the natural and necessary order of science: from elevating the terrestrial, as it were called, above the celestial; and from summoning Reason and Faith to the bar of that limited Physical experience."[4] The visions of science and poetry must remain parallel and complementary ways of seeing, both supporting a dynamic and spiritual conception of life. The rise of a mechanistic science in 1812 became, consequently, a betrayal representative of a trend that had to be countered in every way possible.

Hard on the heels of the disagreements between Coleridge and Davy, the medical controversy of 1814–1819 erupted around issues closely resembling those that separated the two men. The writings of John Hunter catalyzed the debate, whose principal spokesmen were John Abernethy and Sir William Lawrence: Abernethy championed Hunter's spiritual and dynamic principles of life and Lawrence charged that Abernethy's misinterpretations of Hunter were ridiculously unscientific, that Abernethy and his followers arbitrarily and sometimes fantastically used strictly physical phenomena like magnetism or electricity to account for life itself. Abernethy's vital principle, according to Lawrence, was "like a camel, or like a whale, or like what you please."[5] Documenting the main points of this argument in *Coleridge on Logic and Learning*, Alice Snyder notes that the "fundamental questions of the controversy seem to have been two: first, the relation of structure to function; second, the place of theory in physiological investigation—broadly speaking, the method of scientific thought and procedure."[6]

The battle lines on the two questions were clearly drawn. Operating from an avowed theological foundation, Abernethy "could accept no physical science that did violence to his conception of spirit." The life force, he maintained, was independent of organization and structure and prior to it, for the priority of function to structure was essential to the concept of functional unity in any organism. Lawrence, on the other hand, kept his biology and his theology segregated. That an organism was the product of organization was in his view an irrefragable scientific fact, independent of religious questions. Regarding the second question, it is almost needless to point out that Lawrence, the pragmatic laboratory worker, strongly objected to theories and hypotheses and minimized the role of speculation in scientific labor as much as possible. But Abernethy made the most of theory and hypotheses, and "justified them on grounds that suggest the instrumentalist's point of view; he justified them, that is, on grounds of the concrete investigation that they provoked and controlled."[7]

If these were the questions Hunter's work raised and the solutions each faction loudly proclaimed, it goes without saying that both Abernethy and Lawrence discovered in Hunter what they wanted to discover, a way of responding that Coleridge was equally guilty of when he entered the ring of the debate. After rehearsing the quarrel in his "Theory of Life" Coleridge hails Abernethy's role in developing "the true idea of life," a dynamic philosophy like Coleridge's own which gives priority to function over structure and emphasizes the laws of nature rather than the arrangement of particles. "In Mr. Abernethy's Lecture on the Theory of Life," Coleridge writes, "it is impossible not to see a presentiment of a great truth. . . . If the opinions here supported are the same with those of Mr. Abernethy I rejoice in his authority. If they are different, I shall wait with anxious interest for an exposition of that difference."[8] Thoroughly idiosyncratic, "Theory of Life" is Coleridge's defense of Hunter's and Abernethy's vitalism; it attempts to prove and to illustrate that "life itself is not a *thing*—a self-subsistent *hypostasis*—but an *act* and *process*" ("Theory of Life," p. 430). The arrangement of separate bodies or atoms does not explain life; rather, "the most comprehensive formula to which life is reducible, would be that of the internal copula of bodies, or . . . the *power* which discloses itself from within as a principle of *unity* in the *many*" (p. 384). To prove these claims Coleridge presents a detailed outline of the evolution of life as it manifests itself through the conjunction of three forces: magnetism, electricity, and a "chemical affinity." Not surprisingly, each of these forces plays an important role in *Biographia Literaria*.

In its intent and language, "Theory of Life" is clearly a scientific tract, directed at a scientific audience and employing the scientific discourse that Coleridge knew from his attendance at Royal Society lectures and his indefatigable reading of such scientific journals as William Nicholson's *Journal of Natural Philosophy, Chemistry, and the Arts* and the Royal Society's *Philosophical Transactions*.[9] There is some difficulty, of course, in isolating a "scientific discourse" in 1815, since a specialized language for science was only just emerging at this time, just as a specialized thinker called a scientist is only just beginning to be recognized.[10] Coleridge obviously belongs to an earlier tradition that saw the scientist as first of all a natural philosopher, perhaps best described by

the passage from Plato's *Republic* which Coleridge translated as his epigraph to an essay in *The Friend*: "In the following I distinguish, first, those whom indeed you may call
Philotheorists, or Philotechnists, or Practicians, and secondly those whom alone you may rightly denominate *Philosophers*, as knowing what the science of all three branches
of science is, which may prove something more than the
mere aggregate of the knowledge of any particular science."[11]
Nineteenth-century scientists, however, could not be com-
fortable with this archaic, Coleridgean conception of their
role. They needed the precision provided by specialization in
thought and language. So while Coleridge disparaged Davy,
"who seems more and more determined to mould himself
upon the Age in order to make the Age mould itself upon
him,"[12] Davy saw Coleridge's tragedy as a failure to adjust to
the exigencies of modern science. Coleridge's philosophical
language simply lacked the "order, precision, and regularity"
to deal with the problems of contemporary science: "Brilliant images of greatness float upon his mind, like images of
the morning clouds upon the waters. Their forms are changed
by the motions of the waves, they are agitated by every
breeze, and modified by every sunbeam. . . . What talent
does he not waste in forming visions, sublime, but unconnected with the real world!"[13]

Purporting to be more precise and better disciplined, Davy
and his colleagues were isolating themselves in their lab-
oratories and fashioning their own specialized vocabulary.
Hence, whether Coleridge liked the situation or not, if he
wished to argue his philosophy with these men, he had to
learn to use their language. This does not mean that traces of
other discourses, particularly of theology or of alchemy, cannot be found in the scientific vocabulary of 1815. But after
1800, even in Coleridge's writings, scientific discourse sur-
faces with enough autonomy to isolate it, and the "Theory of

Life" is the clearest evidence of Coleridge's own use of that language to defend his beleagured vitalism.

Indeed, translating his science into a modern scientific idiom becomes a major project for Coleridge in 1815, but equally important is the extent to which this scientific model can explain other phenomena, such as art, and how far these other phenomena will corroborate his scientific findings, since implicit in Coleridge's monistic idealism is the common foundation of all areas of knowledge. Coleridge himself never doubts, of course, that there are these links between science and other disciplines. Writing to Tulk in 1817, he says that "true Philosophy . . . takes its roots in Science in order to blossom into Religion,"[14] and in a letter to Lord Liverpool the same year, he recalls his hope that Davy and chemistry will confirm his metaphysics: "If any thing could have recalled the Physics & Physiology of the Age to the Dynamic Theory of the eldest Philosophy, it must have been the late successful researches of the chemists, which almost force on the very senses the facts of mutual penetration and intus-susception which have supplied a series of experimental proofs, that in all pure phaenomena we behold only the copula, the balance or indifference of opposite energies." Moreover, in the same letter, after discussing speculative science, physiology, and "Demiurgic atoms," Coleridge asks, "What is all this to the world at large?" His answer goes some way in explaining why he does not confine scientific language to a scientific treatise, but transfers it to other fields, notably the field of literature in *Biographia Literaria*. Throughout history, Coleridge argues, science or natural philosophy has maintained a direct structural correspondence with other cultural phenomena. "The Taste and Character, the whole tone of Manners and Feelings, and above all the Religious (at least the Theological) and the Political tendencies of the public mind have ever borne such a close correspondence, so distinct and evident an analogy to the predominant system of speculative Philosophy," i.e., natural philosophy or science, that this correspondence "must remain inexplicable, unless we admit not only a reaction and interdependence on both sides, but a powerful, the most indirect influence" of science on the other fields of knowledge. Using examples of art from the medieval period and the eighteenth century, he comments, in a way that might anticipate Michel Foucault, "These are all but the ribs, abutments and sea-marks of a long line of correspondencies in the arts of Taste to the opposite coast of speculative Philosophy."

In short, systems of thought and signification affect the structure of contemporaneous systems, so that an error in a system like speculative philosophy or science could be disseminated throughout other systems. Thus, the "recent relapse . . . of the Chemists to the atomistic scheme, and the almost unanimous acceptance of Dalton's Theory in England, & Le Sage's in France, determine the intellectual character of the age with the force of an *experimentum crucis.*"[15] And even poetry is in danger of being degraded by a mechanistic science whose laws and models will inevitably affect literary criticism and poetry. There is a "link or mordaunt by which philosophy becomes scientific and sciences philosophical,"[16] and likewise there is a link between science and poetry which would allow for the corruption of poetry by science and the substantiation of both through the truth they share. "If in the greatest poets we find Nature idealized through the creative power of a profound yet observant meditation, so through the meditative observation of a Davy, a Wollaston, a Hatchett, or a Murray, . . . we find poetry, as it were, substantiated and realized."[17]

In 1815 Coleridge's task, then, was to establish the connections between his scientific models and the realm of poetry, connections which the scientific community especially were ignoring or denying. From the perspective of Coleridge's visionary philosophy, these connections were clearly present; he needed, however, to substantiate and realize them for the world at large and specifically for his scientific competitors. The solution was in language. Ease and accuracy in transferring the language of "Theory of Life"—the scientist's own inbred tongue—to *Biographia Literaria* became the most direct and effective way of illustrating the commensurability, even the authority, of both Coleridge's science and his poetics.

The way scientific language permeates literary definitions and practical criticism is my primary concern here, and these areas of *Biographia Literaria* generally relate to the issue of function versus arrangement. But the second topic of these debates, the value of theory in investigative research, also plays a large role in the *Biographia*. This second issue is naturally less directly involved with language itself, and has been discussed more frequently by Coleridge scholars than the first issue, though rarely in the context of the medical debates which greatly influenced Coleridge's thinking about theory. Snyder notes that during the medical debates Coleridge

> was forced into a fundamental consideration of the processes of thought. There resulted a vivid realization of the extent to which all thinking is determined by assumptions, ideas, images, and attitudes of even less tangible sorts. Coleridge's insistence that fertilized thinking involved more than induction, and experience more than what is commonly meant to empiricists; that the premises are the critical part of reasoning, and that they depend on something other than the understanding—on a power that brings into play the total man,—these principles of thought and method were formulated through his contacts with many philosophical minds, but to no

THE LANGUAGE OF SCIENCE

small extent their use in the physiological and chemical controversies in which he took part.[18]

More specifically, Coleridge was faced with a choice between Abernethy's method based on theory and Lawrence's method of supposed objectivity based on observation exclusively. He rejected both, however, in favor of his own method based on law, a method derived at least in part from Kant. A scientific definition, Coleridge claims in "Theory of Life," should be neither a theory nor a generalization. It consists

> neither in any single property or function of the thing to be defined, nor yet in all collectively, which latter, indeed, would be a history, not a definition. It must consist, therefore, in the *law* of the thing, or in such an *idea* of it, as being admitted, all the properties and functions are admitted by implication. It must likewise be so far *causal*, that a full insight having been attained of the law, we derive from it a progressive insight into the necessity and *generation* of the phaenomena of which it is the law. (p. 370)

In *Method and Imagination in Coleridge's Criticism*, J. R. de J. Jackson treats fully Coleridge's preference for law over theory, his conclusions usually being correct and usually standard.[19] According to Jackson, the pursuit determines the method; the specific ends determine the means employed. Thus a scientist like Abernethy apprehends truth, "the Communicative Intelligence," through material data, and must rely on the inexact method of theory, which is primarily an educated guess based on prior research. The poet, on the other hand, apprehends intelligence by looking through the material substance to the essence of the phenomena, discovering the law and then presenting the law in the material data of the poem. The poet does not depend on material data for his knowledge. Here Jackson follows Coleridge's thought quite accurately, but his discussion requires two important qualificiations: first, in "Theory of Life" Coleridge argues, in opposition to theoretical scientists, for a scientific method based on law, suggesting therefore the same method for poetry and science; and secondly, in explaining method in Coleridge's theory, Jackson overlooks the reader-critic, whose method is different from the poet's and who is the real subject of *Biographia Literaria*. (If nothing else, the amount of time and space Coleridge uses to berate hack critics tells us that he is discussing a way of investigating poetry, not the way to make a poem, that in the terms of his own distinction he is explaining poetry, not accounting for it.) Though these distinctions may be fine ones, they are very important, for it is in them that the medical debates most obviously make their mark on the *Biographia*. In 1815 the scientific method that Coleridge urges on both Abernethy and Lawrence is one based on law, and accordingly, the critical methodology he proposes and uses in *Biographia Literaria* is the method of law. Both the scientist and the critic work with more or less refined material data, and for both only the method of law can guarantee objectivity and accuracy. In short, though the critic, the poet, and the scientist all search out law, the critic reading the poem is more like the scientist investigating a chemical reaction than like a poet writing a poem.

Investigating poetry in 1815, then, Coleridge works according to a scientific method in which laws are the lamps of good research, and, as is the case in biological research, these laws "of poetry cannot be given from without . . . [but] are the very powers of growth and reproduction,"[20] which the critic must perceive. Here, as in every science, "it is the essence of a scientific definition to be causative, not by introduction of imaginary somewhats, natural or supernatural, under the name of causes, but by announcing the law of action in the particular case, in subordination to the common law of which all phenomena are modifications or results" ("Theory of Life," p. 370). Scientific definitions are causative, not genitive. And in *Biographia Literaria* Coleridge's theoretical definitions do not describe how to make a good poem or propose generalized standards or theories against which to measure a poem. His definitions describe, rather, the laws of poetry as formal causes in every poem, and Coleridge's criticisms of Wordsworth, for instance, point out deviations from these laws. Appropriately, Coleridge's tone and method is that of a biologist noting freakish deviations in the laws of nature. After presenting the laws of poetry—polarity, the secondary imagination, the laws of meter —he examines his material in their light; concentrating on Wordsworth and Shakespeare he *explains* how their works function and where they fall short of the ideal laws of poetry. Thus the organic metaphor does not account for a poem, but explains the ideal laws of its formation. Coleridge is far less concerned with the personality behind the poem—William Wordsworth or William Shakespeare—than with the product those two minds generate.

The issue of theory versus law, however, is only indirectly a product of the scientific language in *Biographia Literaria*. The language itself is a much more immediate and powerful presence, and one of the more effective ways of emphasizing the ubiquitous presence of the scientific language is a simple comparison of passages from the scientific work and the literary work. Since these passages are among Coleridge's most frequently quoted, one well-known example may suffice. In the "Theory of Life" he writes:

> I have shown, moreover, that this tendency to individuate cannot be conceived without the opposite tendency to connect, even as the centrifugal power supposes the centripetal, or as the two opposite poles constitute each

other, and are the constituent acts of one and the same power in the magnet. (p. 391)

And these terms transfer directly to *Biographia Literaria*:

> Bearing this in mind, that intelligence is a self-development, not a quality supervening to a substance, we may abstract from all *degree*, and for the purpose of philosophic construction reduce it to *kind*, under the idea of an indestructable power with two opposite and counteracting forces, which by a metaphor borrowed from astronomy, we may call the centrifugal and centripetal forces. The intelligence in one tends to *objectize* itself, and in those other to know itself in the object. (1:175)

Moreover, some passages in *Biographia Literaria* seem to refer explicitly to the medical debate, using terms which ostensibly have little bearing on literature. This passage from chapter twelve of the *Biographia Literaria* could have been lifted directly from "Theory of Life," though in context it becomes relevant to Coleridge's epistemology and hence his poetics:

> The highest perfection of natural philosophy would consist in the perfect spiritualization of all laws of nature into laws of intuition and intellect. The phaenomena (*the material*) must wholly disappear, and the laws alone (*the formal*) must remain. . . . The optical phaenomena are but a geometry, the lines of which are drawn by light, and the materiality of this light itself has already become a matter of doubt. In the appearances of magnetism all trace of matter is lost, and of the phaenomena of gravitation . . . there remains nothing but its law, the execution of which on a vast scale is the mechanism of the heavenly motions. (1 : 175–76)

Further, Coleridge himself suggests what the evolutionary scheme of "Theory of Life" means to the practicing artist. "Each thing that lives," Coleridge writes in his essay "On Poesy or Art," has "its moment of self-exposition, and so has each period of each thing"; "each step of nature hath its ideal, and . . . the possibility of climax up to the perfect form of a harmonized chaos." Therefore, the "artist must imitate that which is within the thing, that which is active through form and figure, and discourse to us by symbols—the *Naturgeist*, . . . for so only can he hope to produce any work truly natural in the object and truly human in the effect" (*Biographia*, 1:259, 262). Compare this description of imitation to Coleridge's earlier and vaguer distinction between imitation and copying, and it is obvious how his scientific scheme of evolution elaborates and extends that original notion of imitation. The scientific language transforms the earlier simplistic and static definition of imitation as "a combination of certain degree of dissimilitude with a certain degree of similitude"[21] into a more dynamic, evolutionary concept that anticipates the pseudo-scientific poetics of Hulme and others.

A final and more concrete example of Coleridge's transferring scientific discourse to the definitions and literary principles in *Biographia Literaria* is his description of genius, specifically of Wordsworth's genius. Out of context the statement on Wordsworth's development seems an ungainly simile; however, in the context of the medical debate whose occasion and primary issue was the nature of physiological disorders and diseases, the language reverberates with a special biological significance.

It is remarkable how soon genius clears and purifies itself from the faults and errors of its earliest products; faults which, in its earliest compositions, are the more obtrusive and confluent, because as heterogenous elements, which had only a temporary use, they constitute the very *ferment*, by which they themselves are carried off. Or we may compare them to some diseases, which must work on humours, and be thrown out on the surface, in order to secure the patient from their future recurrence. (1:57–58)

Here Coleridge's language makes meaning as it suggests a rather peculiar, biological understanding of how genius develops and how artistic faults correct themselves. Express this idea in different terms and a different idea takes its place. Discussing Coleridge's use of the word *polarity*, J. Isaacs makes the same point:

> First of all, by his underlining of the word, it is clear that Coleridge is either proud of his invention of it, or regards it as a significant and careful use; secondly, the word is a valuable contribution to our critical armoury, and its uses have not yet been exhausted; thirdly, the O.E.D. can find no earlier use of the term in this special shade of usage; fourthly, it is clear from his reference to "the polarity of the magnet," in the same encyclopedia article on "Method," that this is not merely a loose employment of the normal use of the word; and lastly, the fact that this use is a subtle and thought-out transference of a term to the great central problem of Coleridge's researches into the esemplastic power, the coadunating faculty, and the problem of multeity in unity, gives an emotional significance of the highest order to this otherwise cold technical term.[23]

In each of these examples I am drawing attention to the scientific language itself as the formative agent in Coleridge's pronouncements on literature. Hence, my position is opposite to that of most critics who view the scientific language as a metaphor in a monistic system that merges different terminologies. Coleridge's monistic vision is undeniable, but the scientific discourse is clearly more than metaphoric—or at least metaphors and similes have a greater role and a more complicated function than most critics have observed in the past. If Coleridge's vision is monistic, his understanding is pluralistic.

In a recent article Jonathan Culler makes a similar point about the connotative power and cultural significance of two of Coleridge's most important critical terms, *allegory* and *symbol*. Along with Culler's other work, this article is particularly important because it leads the way in indicating how a linguistic focus can unveil the structural makeup of Coleridge's critical writings and delineate the historical, cultural codes that are the foundation of these writings. Culler begins his analysis of Coleridge by describing the structural differences that distinguish an allegorical sign from a symbolic sign. "The allegorical sign, we might say, is arbitrary: the connection between signifier and signified is imposed by the mind or fancy, while the eye and imagination are aware primarily of the difference. The symbol, on the other hand, is a motivated sign, a synecdoche, in which the signifier is naturally connected to the signified." The distinction relates, in turn, to the opposition between mechanical and organic form:

Allegory for Coleridge is an instance of "mechanic form," of a deliberate yoking together of the heterogeneous, whereas the symbol is a case of "organic form" based on the intuitive grasp of natural relationship. The symbol achieves a fusion of subject and object because in the symbol the truth of the subject or perceiver is also the truth of the object, its natural significance. In allegory, on the other hand, one remains aware of the irreducible difference between the object itself as signifier and the meaning imposed by the fancy of the subject.[23]

We have here two fundamental tropes or codes, "two ways of organizing the attribution of meaning." And according to Culler, a general doctrinal or cultural "shift in formal operations for the production of meaning" accounts for Coleridge's preference for the symbolic.

Culler, I believe, overstates this last point, for this shift in the operations for the production of meaning is less an undefined doctrinal shift than a product of contemporary scientific discourse and an organismic trope. That is, Coleridge's preference for the symbolic is, above all else, connected with scientific issues and scientific language of his day, which Culler explains in terms of the semantic shifts then taking place: "In the discourse of natural history Michel Foucault has traced the movement which leads from classical taxonomy, in which observable differences and similarities between plants and animals are reflected in a corresponding order of names, to the new botany and biology in which hidden properties become the most significant and the true defining characteristics of the organism. . . . The new organism tries, as Cuvier wrote, to establish the correspondence between exterior and interior forms which are all integral parts of the animal's essence; significance is what can be drawn from within the organism itself."[24] Many other fields of knowledge, such as history, were undergoing similar changes in epistemology, but science was clearly providing the key terms and the structures according to which meaning was assigned. My point is this: formal operations in language do not change "generally," as Culler says, but alter because of changes in the operations of a specific discourse which, in turn, affect the formal operations in the discourses surrounding it. Such is the case here, and Culler, perhaps unwittingly, confirms this when he depends on the biological term *organism* to denote the linguistic shift in other discourses such as history.

Coleridge's 1816 distinction between allegory and symbol is one of his most famous critical definitions and tools; the extent to which its significance derives from and depends on Coleridge's scientific discourse is indicative of many of his literary maxims at this time. I have already shown how in a number of places his scientific language transfers directly to a literary context, resulting in principles for criticism that have made Coleridge famous and infamous at once. In those examples, the scientific language provides definitions or codes explicitly meant to organize the attribution of meaning in literature, so that reading a poem as either allegorical or symbolic has important repercussions regarding how and what the poem means. Far less explicitly the scientific discourse controls much of the practical criticism of *Biographia Literaria*, and though scientific language often has little bearing on Coleridge's descriptions and judgments of Wordsworth's poetry, just as often these critical interpretations are made by means of a scientific code or model which supplements the primary text and produces a kind of meaning one would be hard pressed to locate in Wordsworth's poetry. The features of the text which this scientific language selects for interpretation are naturally predetermined by the model itself, and a scientific terminology which has been arguing the priority of function over arrangement to a medical audience will accordingly be directed at the formal features of a poem.

So much has been written about Coleridge's formal criticism and his organic model that it is not necessary to rehash points that have become commonplaces. Worthy of attention, though, are the elaborations on that trope which follow from Coleridge's more subtle thinking about science in 1815, and the way these elaborations manifest themselves in the practical criticism of *Biographia Literaria*. For instance, Coleridge's grounds for differentiating poetry and prose, the first truly practical problem in the *Biographia*, immediately recalls the first issue of the medical controversy:

> A poem contains the same elements as a prose composition; the difference therefore must consist in a different combination of them, in consequence of a different object being proposed. According to the difference of the object will be the difference of the combination. It is possible, that the object may be merely to facilitate the recollection of any given facts or observations by artificial arrangement; and the composition will be a poem, merely because it is distinguished from prose by meter, or by rhyme, or by both conjointly. (2:8)

In short, what differentiates poetry and prose is not mere arrangement of "elements," as the mechanistic scientists would argue, but the function of the two forms, the "object being proposed" by each.

The emphasis on function over arrangement informs the vast majority of critical judgments in *Biographia Literaria*, and as Coleridge attempts to employ this formula in different and more subtle ways when analyzing poems, scientific tropes and biological descriptions more overtly prejudice the judgments. In fact, biological descriptions and connotations are so ubiquitous that the scientific world of plants and organisms merges with the literary world. Differentiating Wordsworth's and Coleridge's natural world, Abrams notes that the nature Coleridge "ultimately appeals to in art is basically a biological nature," and it "is astonishing how much of Coleridge's critical writing is couched in terms that are metaphorical for art and literal for plants. . . . Only let the vehicle of his metaphors come alive, and you see all the objects of criticism writhe surrealistically into plants or parts of plants, growing in tropical profusion."[25] Indeed Coleridge's prefatory statement on Wordsworth's "Descriptive Sketches" is a description of an organic jungle:

> Seldom, if ever, was the emergence of an original genius above the literary horizon more evidently announced. In the form, style, and manner of the whole poem, and in the structure of particular lines and periods, there is an *harshness* and *acerbity* connected and combined with words and images *all a-glow*, which might recall *those products of the vegetable world*, where *gorgeous blossoms* rise out of the *hard* and *thorny rind* and *shell*, within which the *rich fruit* was elaborating. The language was not only peculiar and strong, but at times *knotty* and *contorted*, as by its own *impatient strength*. (*Biographia*, 1:56; my emphasis)

Later, he lists as the third and fourth excellences of Wordsworth's poetry "the sinewy strength and originality of single lines and paragraphs . . . the perfect truth of nature in his images and descriptions, as taken immediately from nature, and proving a long and genial intimacy with the very spirit which gives the *physiognomic expression* to all works of nature" (2 : 121). And finally, "as a sort of allegory, or connected simile and metaphor of Wordsworth's intellect and genius," Coleridge quotes *Bartram's Travels*: "The soil is a deep, rich, dark mould, on a deep stratum of tenacious clay; and that on a foundation of rocks, which often break through both strata, lifting their back above the surface. The trees which chiefly grow here are the gigantic black oak; magnolia magni-flora; fainus excelsior; platane; and a few stately tulip trees" (2:128–29). Three years after these statements Coleridge called Shakespeare a "comparative anatomist" who "works from within by evolution and assimilation" and produces beautiful fruits. By contrast, Beaumont and Fletcher "took from the ear and eye, unchecked by any intuition of an inward possibility, just as a man might fit together a quarter of an orange, a quarter of an apple, and the like of a lemon and of a pomegranate, and make it look like one round diverse colored fruit."[26]

Although Abrams hesitates to admit it and Coleridge himself back-pedals by asking pardon for the terms borrowed from chemistry and botany, he clearly intended Wordsworth's and Shakespeare's poetry literally to come alive and be seen as a living organism. Poetic language can never actually have a "physiognomic expression," but Coleridge's critical language can attribute it to Wordsworth's and Shakespeare's poetry, by using a biological language to connote and signify a biological signified. Abrams himself suggests this productive power when in *The Mirror and the Lamp* he explains how critical metaphors and analogies are often not simply illustrative but constitutive. This is certainly the case here, where Coleridge's scientific language reconstructs poetry as a living organism, a three-dimensional object, which functions in much the same way as his plants, animals, and men in "Theory of Life." Pater, I believe, is more correct than most critics admit when he complains of Coleridge's identifying the poem with an actual plant; in *Biographia Literaria* Coleridge certainly exaggerates the case this way. He may, as critics have traditionally observed, be concerned with the creative process, the subjective nature of poetry, but in the *Biographia* that process is objectified, presented as a product, by using a scientific language which transforms the forces of the process into forces of a product. The language is much more elusive in *Biographia Literaria* than in "Theory of Life," but it is quite clear that the forces operative in a poem correlate directly with the three forces of nature: magnetism, electricity, and chemical affinity. There is, in other words, a six-part homology established between the world of biology and the world of poetry. The great value in transferring this three-part model from science to poetry is that Coleridge could use it to distinguish different operations in a poem while implicitly suggesting their unity on the evidence that, as in the biological example in "Theory of Life," "the lower powers are assimilated, not merely employed—which presupposes homogeneity" ("Theory of Life," p. 386).

Of the three powers which Coleridge describes in "Theory of Life," magnetism or polarity is the most prominent. In that treatise Coleridge makes it clear that, as the most basic force in nature, magnetism is the first expression of the polarity principle, and in this state it is predominantly mechanical, "two equal forces acting in opposite directions" (*Biographia*, 1:197). Barfield, without doubt the most lucid explicator of polarity, makes the crucial point that the mechanical *law* of polarity must be distinguished from the *power* of polarity, for if magnetism is an essentially mechanical law, it eventually becomes assimilated into a higher power that is essentially dynamic. Coleridge explains this relative nature of magnetism towards the conclusion of "Theory of Life": "Relatively . . . to fluidity, that is, to matter, the parts of which cannot be distinguished from each other by figure, magnetism is the power of fixity: but, relatively to itself, magnetism . . . is designated by its opposite poles, and must be represented as the magnetic axis, the northern pole of which signifies rest, attraction, fixity, coherence, or hardness; . . . while the southern pole, as its antithesis, represents mobility, repulsion, incoherence, and fusibility" (p. 408).

In their most primitive form, before their conversion into a vital power, the poles of a magnet provide an object with fixity: the magnetic poles are "the primary constituent *Powers*."[27] As Seth Watson observes in his introduction to "Theory of Life," magnetism thus becomes the "first and simplest differential act of Nature . . . the first step from indifference to difference, from formless homogeneity to independent ex-

145

istence" (p. 360). In a poem this rudimentary act of fixity and differentiation is described by the famous pairs that constitute all poems and that become objectified elements in the poem—"sameness with difference; of the general, with the concrete; the idea, with the image; the individual, with the representative; the sense of novelty and freshness, with old and familiar objects; a more than usual state of emotion, with more than usual order" (*Biographia*, 2:12). These poles differentiate a poem, define it, and balance it, as it were, in a fixed position. Balance, in fact, is the key to the polar arrangement in a poem, just as it is in a magnet, for "in all pure phaenomena we behold only the copula, the balance or indifference of opposite energies."[28] Accordingly, where Wordsworth's feelings are "disproportionate to *such* knowledge and value of objects described" the stability of the poem is upset; accusing Wordsworth of mental bombast is a criticism of misbalanced energies. (2:109). Likewise, Coleridge complains of metaphysical poets and some of his contemporaries who in different ways destroy the balance needed in a poem. "Our faulty elder poets sacrificed the passion and passionate flow of poetry to the subtleties of intellect, and to the starts of wit; the moderns to the glare and glitter of a perpetual, yet broken and heterogeneous imagery, or rather to an amphibious something, made up, half of image, and half of abstract meaning. The one sacrificed the heart to the head; the other both heart and head to point and drapery" (1:15).

Because Coleridge himself rarely dissected his polarity principle and only in "Theory of Life" and his long letter to Tulk in 1817 made a sustained attempt to show clearly how it relates to the magnetic law as opposed to the electrical power, critics often confuse the polarity of magnetism and the polarity of electricity. But in order to fully understand the intricacies of the criticism in *Biographia Literaria*, and especially the role of imagination, one must be aware of these finer distinctions. Again, polarity is the first law of nature, and magnetism's property of attraction and repulsion is the first manifestation of that law. But the two poles of magnetism generate a second force, electricity, which simultaneously vitalizes the fixed magnetic field and stands as the polar opposite to magnetism. (Magnetism and electricity become intersecting axes, each axis having two poles.) In Coleridge's evolutionary scheme, the magnetic force manifests itself most obviously in inorganic metals, and later, when the electrical force becomes predominant, vegetable life and insects appear. Thus, from the conjunction of electricity and magnetism, in various proportions, the different forms of life are made. In the arrangement, represented by the magnetic poles, "life subsists"; in their strife, represented by electricity, "it consists" ("Theory of Life," p. 393).

The addition of this second power to Coleridge's scientific scheme should never be underestimated. Seth Watson went so far as to say that electricity was "the foundation of life" for Coleridge. This is of course incorrect, a point Coleridge made abundantly clear in "Theory of Life." Yet electricity did provide an illustration and scientific solution to the burden of magnetism and its association with lifeless arrangement. A "new light was struck by the discovery of electricity, and in every sense of the word, . . . it may be affirmed to have electrified the whole frame of natural philosophy" (p. 375). Electricity was a power that could convert the static arrangement of the magnetic field into a space of vital action and movement, and sometime around 1816 Coleridge added a long passage to the revised *Friend*, hailing contemporary research in electricity. After discussing the work of Hunter and Abernethy, Coleridge remarks that all theories of electricity have in common

the idea of *two-opposite-forces*, tending to rest by equilibrium. These are the sole factors of the calculus, alike in all theories. These give the *law*, and in it the *method*, both of arranging the phaenomena and of substantiating appearances into facts of science. . . . For this reason, we anticipate the greatest improvements in the *method*, the nearest approaches to a *system* of electricity from these philosophers, who have presented the law most purely, and the correlative idea as an idea: those, namely, who, since the year 1798, in the true spirit of experimental dynamic, rejecting the imagination of any material substrate, simple or compound, contemplate in the phaenomena of electricity the operation of a law which reigns through all nature, the law of POLARITY, or the manifestation of one power by opposite forces: who trace in these appearances, as the most obvious and striking of its innumerable forms, the agency of the positive and negative poles of a power essential to all material construction; the second, namely, of the three primary principles, for which the beautiful and most appropriate symbols are given by the mind in the three ideal dimensions of space.[29]

Method, for Coleridge, is invariably equated with a unifying process and here it is associated with "a system of electricity" which illustrates the one power operating according to the law of polarity. Magnetism, that is, can represent the law of polarity; electricity the vitalization or operation of that law. If magnetism demonstrated the law of polarity in inorganic matter, electricity assimilated magnetism to reveal the one power that brings polarity to life in organic matter. The principle of fixity fuses with the principle of dynamic motion; or, as he phrases it in a description of artistic beauty, "confining form" unites with the "electrical flashes" of "free life."[30]

In the *Biographia Literaria* the imagination is an objectified power within the poem, and as such, it is the counterpart to the electrical power in nature described in "Theory of

Life." The scientific language with which it is described is indicative of this correspondence: "The primary imagination I hold to be the *living Power* and *prime Agent* of all human Perception. . . . The secondary Imagination I consider as an echo of the former, co-existing with the conscious will, yet still as identical with the primary in *the kind of its agency*, and differing only in degree, and in *the mode of its operation*. It *dissolves*, *diffuses*, and dissipates, in order to recreate. . . . It is essentially *vital*, even as objects (*as objects*) are essentially fixed and dead" (*Biographia*, 1:202; my emphasis). "This power, first put in action by the will and understanding, and retained under their irremissive, though gentle and unnoticed control . . . reveals itself in the balance or reconciliation of opposite or discordant qualities" (2:12). Here the language is that of a scientific experiment in which an electrical force, the imagination, galvanizes different elements that are brought under its power: working together, the will and understanding act as a conductor that organizes a field of "opposite and discordant qualities" which the fusing power of the imagination vitalizes in a manner strikingly similar to the operation of the electrical force found in nature. Shakespeare's work is thus a "growth, evolution" whereby "each line, each word almost, begets the following—and the will of the writer is in interfusion, a continuous agency, no series of separate acts."[31] The conducting will unites with the fusing imagination to become "an interfusion, a continuous agency" of power and control that at once organizes and activates the multiple elements of a wide and varied experience.

The clearest use of electricity in practical criticism, however, is found in Coleridge's analysis of meter. He begins by describing the origins of meter, tracing it "to the balance of the mind effected by the spontaneous effort which strives to hold in check the workings of passion. It might be easily explained likewise in what manner this salutary antagonism is assisted by the very state which it counteracts; and how this balance of antagonists becomes organized into *meter* . . . by a supervening act of the will and judgment" (2:49–50). Meter, that is, generated out of a polarity of passion and the controlling effort of the mind that, like the magnetic field, together form a balance of antagonists between which the will intervenes like a conductor. Metrical restraint is then balanced with a language of passion: "As every passion has its proper pulse, so it will likewise have its characteristic mode of expression" (2:56). In short, mental restraint and passion balance in an original act of the mind that results in meter; to create poetry, this metrical framework is in turn bound and balanced with a special, emotional language: "Meter therefore having been connected with *poetry* most often and by a peculiar fitness, whatever else is combined with *meter* must, though it not be *essentially* poetic, have nevertheless some property in common with poetry, as an intermedium of affinity, a sort (if I may dare borrow a well-known phrase from technical chemistry) of *mordaunt* between it and the super-added meter" (2:55). The suggestion here, which could be made only through the scientific language in which it is couched, is that meter can be either an artificial or natural part of a poem in that "an intermedium of affinity" should *naturally* bind meter to the language of a poem. And although Coleridge never explicitly explains it in terms of the imagination, it seems clear that what activates this affinity is the imagination that he consistently describes, with similar scientific language, as the power that vitalizes and unites contrary elements. Where Coleridge fails to discover this balance and conjunction between the language of the poetry and the meter, in Wordsworth's "Anecdote for Fathers," "Simon Lee," "Alice Fell," "The Beggars," and "The Sailor's Mother," he rightly claims that these poems "would have been delightful . . . in prose, told and managed, as by Mr. Wordsworth they would have been, in a moral essay, or pedestrian tour" (2:53). About "The Sailor's Mother" specifically, he quotes three stanzas and queries "whether in the *metre* itself he found a sufficient reason for *their* being written metrically?" (2:54), tacitly referring here, I believe, to the model he has established whereby there must be a vitalized affinity between the meter and the language of the poem. As the two are joined but not imaginatively united in the Wordsworth poem, the meter sits oddly on the language of the poem, just as the leaves of one flower would look strange if unnaturally grafted on the stem of another species.

In "Theory of Life" Coleridge also discusses magnetism and electricity in terms of "progressive individuation," and this concept too bears on evaluations and judgments in *Biographia Literaria*. In nature, "the unceasing polarity of life" represented by magnetism, Coleridge writes, is "the form of its progress, and its tendency to progressive individuation" is "the law of its direction" ("Theory of Life," p. 407). Here magnetic polarity describes the form, and what I have associated with the imagination (in art) and the electrical force (in nature), namely, the process within the form, now becomes "the tendency to progressive individuation." One of the two principal ideas in "Theory of Life," progressive individuation implies two movements which are represented by the poles of the electrical axis, the centripetal and centrifugal powers: "This tendency to individuate cannot be conceived without the opposite tendency to connect, even as the centrifugal power supposes the centripetal. . . . Again, if the tendency be at once to individuate and to connect, to detach, but so as either to retain or to reproduce attachment, the individuation itself must be a tendency to the ultimate production of the highest and most comprehensive individuality" (p. 391). Progressive individuation embraces two counteracting tendencies in nature, "that of *detachment* from the universal life . . . and that of attachment or reduction into it" (p. 389), both of which reappear in the *Biographia* and the related essays in the term "multeity in unity," a term whose definition almost always approximates the definition of progressive individuation. In his essay "On Poesy or Art," Coleridge comments that the pleasure of art "consists in the identity of two opposite elements, that is to say—sameness and variety. . . . In order to derive pleasure from the occupation of the mind, the principle of unity must always be present, so that in the midst of the multeity the centripetal force be never suspended, nor the sense be fatigued by the predominance of the centrifugal force. This unity in multeity I have elsewhere stated as the principle of beauty" (*Biographia*, 2:262). And, early in *Biographia Literaria*, Coleridge lays the groundwork for differentiating kinds of creative minds by distinguishing the centrifugal and centripetal forces in the mind: "The intelligence in the one tends to *objectize* itself, and in the other to know itself in the object" (1:188).

Whether Coleridge is talking about the creative process of art or the forces of nature, the significance of the language remains the same in each of these passages. As the progressive individuation manifested in the electrical force unites and vitalizes two opposite movements in the life process, in poetry the imagination performs the same task. Though Coleridge never bluntly states this, he values a work of art most when its centrifugal-centripetal make-up resembles man, the organism in whom the two forces reach their maximum strength and scope. In nature, Coleridge says, "the tendency to individuation . . . constitutes the common character of all classes," and "the degrees both of intensity and extension, to which this tendency is realized, form the species, and their ranks, in the great scale of ascent and expansion" ("Theory of Life," p. 390). On this scale, the higher, more complex organisms are the ones in which more individuality unites with more universality or variety of parts, and "the individuality is most intense where the greatest dependence of the parts or the whole is combined with the greatest dependence of the whole on the parts." The pinnacle of this scale is man, for man is the "highest realization and reconciliation of both . . . tendencies, that of most perfect detachment and the greatest possible union" (p. 422). In man the "whole force of organic power has attained an inward and centripetal direction. He has the whole world in counterpoint to him, but he contains an entire world within himself (p. 423).

Accordingly, if the paramount, most admirable organism is the one that manifests the most detachment with the greatest attachment, in literature most value will be awarded to the work that manifests the greatest individuality with the greatest universality. The works of Shakespeare and Milton are Coleridge's examples here.[32] Shakespeare's plays not only have a universal scope and variety, but also contain a proportionate degree of judgment and unity. "In Shakespeare the play is *syngenesia* a flower species—each indeed has a life of its own and is an individuum of itself, but yet an organ to the whole."[33] Conversely, while always retaining the stamp of the individual man, the poems of Milton contain the greatest of eternal truths. Wordsworth too is praised as "individualized," but his characters, unlike Shakespeare's, are faulted as overly peculiar and "incongruous," "for amid the strongest individuation, the character must still remain representative" (*Biographia*, 2:106–7). Finally, the great philosophical poem that Coleridge expected from Wordsworth would doubtless have been great because, like man, the scope of its vision would have been matched by the strength of its individuality.

I have discussed progressive individuation in its relation to the second power in Coleridge's biological scheme—electricity in nature and the imagination in poetry—since Coleridge most usually associates it with these two phenomena. Yet, as all three powers are bound together in a single organism, so the tendency to individuate cannot be separated from the third power, chemical affinity, which corresponds to the intellectual energy and reason behind a poem. Chemical affinity adds the dimension of depth to an organism when it unites with length and breadth, magnetism and electricity, and in "Theory of Life" Coleridge equates chemical affinity with sensibility. He describes this third dimension best in a manuscript note:

> All that is *outside* is comprized in length and surface—what remains must therefore be *inside*—but again, the sole definition of matter is that which fills space—now it is with length, breadth, and length relative to Breadth that space is filled. In other words, Space has relation only to the outside. Depth must therefore be that *by* not *with* which space is filled . . . it must be that which causes it to be filled, and is therefore the true substance. Depth therefore cannot be an attribute of matter, which (i.e. Length + Breadth or Extension) is itself a mere abstraction, an ens rationis; but it must be a Power, the essence of which is *inwardness*, outwardness being its effect and mode of manifesting itself.[34]

Illustrating inwardness, "the true substance," in a poem will always be a perilous task for a critic, but nonetheless Coleridge attempts it, if somewhat coyly, by locating a particular kind of sensibility in a poem. He praises the "atmosphere and depth and height" of Wordsworth's poetic world, and he characterizes the fifth of Wordsworth's excellences, a meditative pathos, as "a union of deep and subtle thought with sensibility" (*Biographia*, 2:122). For Coleridge this is an important and positive criticism of Wordsworth, and it correlates neatly with the third dimension of an organism—depth, sensibility, and inwardness of thought. An elusive and protean presence but one which most readers are aware of and recognize in a poem, "thought" is perhaps as specific as Coleridge can be about a third-dimensional property in a poem. But how to show it working in a poem is extremely difficult, which accounts for how comparatively little Coleridge says about depth in a poem. As a power in the poem it dwells in the realm of Coleridge's reason and philosophical Ideas, clearly distinguished from the imaginative power, so that, besides imagination, Shakespeare possesses another poetic power "without which the former could scarce exist in a high degree," namely, "Depth and Energy of Thought" (2:19). In an 1818 lecture, Coleridge describes the conjunction of these two powers, imaginative force and depth, this way: Shakespeare "worked in the spirit of nature, by evolving the germ within the imaginative power according to an idea." For "no man was ever yet a great poet, without being at the same time a profound philosopher. . . . In Shakespeare's poems the creative power and the intellectual energy wrestle as in a war embrace" (2:19). The thinker, as well as the imaginative artist, adds a dimension to the poem, so that balance, imagination, and energy of thought unite in a poem, like electricity, magnetism, and chemical affinity in the life process, to create an object that is as complicated and mysterious as the highest organism in nature.

Just as Coleridge never forgets this ultimately mysterious nature of art and life no matter how analytical he becomes, so his three-dimensional model should never be confused with poetic truth and life itself. If the constituent forces of life are the power of length (magnetism), the power of surface (electricity), and the power of depth (chemical affinity), "life itself is neither of these separately, but the copula of all three" ("Theory of Life," p. 430). Indeed the powers of life may manifest themselves in concrete comprehensible forms, yet "visible surface and *power* of any kind, much more the *power* of life, are ideas which the forms of human understanding make it impossible to identify" (p. 378). Likewise, the living truth of a poem exists beyond the components Coleridge chooses to isolate for criticism, and a critic's most egregious mistake would be to imagine Wordsworth's or any author's poetry simple and containable.

What Coleridge and other literary critics can do is to understand and explain life and poetry with language. Precisely because of its linguistic nature, this act of understanding will always be an act of commitment and choice—a choice of how they will understand and, subsequently, what they will understand. Scientific language does not appear accidentally or inadvertently in *Biographia Literaria*; it is the controlling discourse that Coleridge chooses for good reasons and with full knowledge of its implications. He recognizes the power of connotations; he recognizes the way different tropes and metaphors could not only organize but produce meanings. He writes about a "fusing power" in a poem, entirely conscious of its commensurability with the "fusing power" of electricity. And, describing "depth" in a poem or its centripetal-centrifugal balance, Coleridge consciously creates a meaning, a biological meaning, rather than extracting that meaning from a poem. In 1815 the language of science was gaining an authority that could only diminish the authority of other languages: due to the purported objectivity of scientific practice and discourse, scientific statements simply had more validity than poetic or theological statements. For Coleridge, the way to counter this trend was to make a poem *mean* scientifically, to show that scientific truths are not confined to science any more than scientific discourse is the sole property of the theoretical physicist. If poetry should never pretend to be science, it should also never cower before the language of science. Coleridge's scientific poetics and biological tropes are an important attempt to show that poetry is at least as challenging, mysterious, and intellectually rigorous as the best of modern science.

CHAPTER FIVE

Accommodating Aeschylus: Coleridge, Theology, and Literary Criticism

This I believe by my own dear experience,—that the more tranquilly an inquirer takes up the Bible as he would any other body of writings, the livelier and steadier will be his impressions of its superiority to all other books, till at length all other books and all other knowledge will be valuable in his eyes in proportion as they help him to better understand his Bible.

COLERIDGE,
Confessions of an Inquiring Spirit

Delivered in May 1825 to the Royal Society of Literature, Coleridge's lecture "On the *Prometheus* of Aeschylus" must certainly have puzzled its first audience as much as it has confused its few readers since then.[1] Indeed Coleridge seemed to recognize this fact when he wrote John Taylor Coleridge the next day that he "inflicted the whole Essay (an hour and 25 M) on the ears of the R.L.S., with most remorseful sympathy with the audience, who could not possibly understand the 10th part."[2] Here, as usual, part of Coleridge's problem was that he had simply packed too much dense material into too small a space. But, more important for my argument, this puzzlement and difficulty follow from what Carlyle disdainfully called the "swimbladders and vehiculatory gears" that overwhelm a lecture purportedly on Aeschylus's *Prometheus*.

There is, in short, only a polite nod to Aeschylus's play in this lecture, while the vast majority of it grinds out a discussion of theology and theological history, using *Prometheus* merely as a vehicle for Coleridge's involved theological models. Particularly in this essay Coleridge's commentary explodes around the primary text, often leaving that text unrecognizable or buried in the critical commentary that covers it. It takes to an extreme a method of reading and criticizing that I have been tracing throughout Coleridge's career, a method whereby a specific extraliterary code—here theological—interacts with a primary text not simply to rephrase its meaning but in fact to *produce* a meaning. In the earlier years this method is less obvious for many reasons. In the last years, it is unmistakably evident, making Aeschylus's play into a rather bare grid upon which Coleridge charts his own ideas about theology and theological history. To be sure, at no period in Coleridge's life does his literary criticism purport only to be at the service of a literary work that arrived first: almost always a particular discourse—political, scientific, or psychological, for example—controls Coleridge's criticism and contributes significantly to the meaning of a primary text. In these final years, however, the conspiracy of the commentary against the text is overwhelming. What is most peculiar about his work during this period is the unusual extent to which he disregards the primary text and how completely his complex theological models and language usurp that text. In the *Prometheus* lecture particularly Coleridge tacitly claims that another text, a theological one, has precedence over all other literature; this theological text is always primary; and it thus determines not only the meaning of a literary work but even the literature that is worth reading. Annotating Milton's minor poems in the 1820s, Coleridge explains this new hierarchy of texts clearly: "Of criticism we may perhaps say, that those divine poets, Homer, Eschylus, and the two compeers, Dante, Shakespeare, Spenser, Milton, who deserve to have Critics, . . . are placed above criticism in the vulgar sense, and move in the sphere of religion, while those who are not such scarcely deserve criticism in any sense."[3] Never descending to vulgar criticism, Coleridge's literary criticism in the 1820s invariably moves in this sphere of religion. And to understand it, the otherwise baffled reader needs to know far less about the meaning of a specific poem or play than about the meaning of a theological language that massively invades and controls the literary commentary.

THIS VICTORY OF THEOLOGICAL DISCOURSE over literature proper in Coleridge's last years is not really surprising, since from 1818 to 1834 theology dominates Coleridge's work more and more until it becomes the almost exclusive passion of his life. As J. Robert Barth observes, after the completion of the *Biographia Literaria* "Coleridge continued through the next several years to speak and write occasionally about literary subjects, . . . but there was a noticeable change of his emphasis in his work, until by 1819 we find that he had turned his attention rather completely to other things. . . . This change in the bent of his work˙ . . . was strongly in the direction of religious preoccupations."[4] Theology is of course central to Coleridge's life from his earliest days through his old age, but the changing meaning of theology and religion at different periods of his life is crucial to a proper understanding of his work. In the 1790s, for instance, theology and religious thought are usually the handmaiden of a rather topical, practical morality, and the disciple of William Frend and editor of *The Watchman* is certainly a religious thinker of a different sort than the Coleridge of the 1820s, whose interest in politics is always subordinate to theological models and laws. Hence, though they ostensibly deal with a similar topic—the relation between politics and theology—*On the Constitution of the Church and State* is fundamentally different from the *Lectures 1795 on Politics and Religion*. Both the language and overriding vision have changed, so that whereas in the earlier work Christ appears as a political revolutionary of sorts, in the later work the political state must serve God's plan. Indeed these last fifteen years of Coleridge's life mark his most whole-hearted and nearly exclusive commitment to theology, and his writings

during this period testify to his increasingly abstract thinking in this area, thinking demanded both by Coleridge's private needs and by his awareness of a historical crisis in
which the spirit of practiced religion was being demeaned by
a new breed of rationalists. *Aids to Reflection* and *Church
and State*, the most famous products of this period in Coleridge's life, put the case most strongly. But his poetry too is
clearly more a vehicle for expounding speculative, mostly
orthodox theology than for dramatizing the concrete questions or problems that concerned him as a young man; after
1820, the reproof of Sara in "The Aeolian Harp" is no longer
necessary.[5]

As Coleridge immerses himself in theology during these
years, one of the salient issues becomes scriptural hermeneutics, an issue that bears very significantly on his interpretations of literature. *Confessions of an Inquiring Spirit*, a
third prose work written during these years, deals with this
issue most directly, and the incisiveness with which Coleridge discusses hermeneutics and the provocativeness of
these remarks make it a central document in an understanding of his later literary criticism. The occasion for this short,
posthumously published work is the debates and controversies about how the Bible should be read. One camp in this
controversy, the "biblical rationalists," with whom Herder is
often identified, stresses the human and historical dimension of the Scriptures, and, frequently taking the argument
to an extreme, tends to deny the divine origin and authority
of the Bible; opposing the rationalists are the strict orthodox
thinkers who adhere to some version of divine ventrilo-
quism, maintaining that every word of the Bible is the infallible word of God, and sometimes subsequently finding their
interpretations challenged by scientific or historical facts.

As usual, Coleridge is not willing to throw his unqualified
support to either side. Instead he proposes a kind of biblical
exegesis which stands midway between the two extremes:

for Coleridge there is never any doubt about the divine origin of the Bible, and to denigrate it as fiction or to deny its authority is blasphemy; yet the infinite qualitative difference between God and man, along with the inherent limitations of language, makes it silly to believe in the literal infallibility of the Bible's written message.[6] "How can infallible truth be conveyed in defective material?" Coleridge asks. God is doubtless the infallible intelligence behind the Scriptures, but the vehicles for this message are fallible man and a language that is defective by its nature. Summing up his position in the argument, Coleridge writes:

> There is a Light higher than all . . . the Light, of which light itself is but the *schechinah* and cloudy tabernacle;—the Word that is light for every man, and light for as many as give heed to it. If between this Word and the written Letter I shall anywhere seem to myself to find a discrepance, I shall not conclude that such there actually is; nor on the other hand will I fall under the condemnation of them that would *lie for God*, but seek as I may, be thankful for what I have and wait.[7]

Moreover, not only is there a gap between the divine meaning and the words which are its vehicles, but the interpreters of those words are no less subject to error. "Every sentence found in a canonical Book, rightly interpreted," Coleridge writes, "contains the *dictum* of an infallible Mind; but what the right interpretation is,—or whether the very words now extant are corrupt or genuine—must be determined by the industry and understanding of the fallible and alas! more or less prejudiced theologians" (*Confessions*, pp. 53–54). The Scriptures, in other words, convey a profound spiritual meaning which is not always in accord with the strict literal meaning of the language used to convey that message. To read it correctly, then, the interpreter must read with spiritual eyes that discover the moral sense, not with physical eyes that are invariably distracted by literal sense. False interpretation derives either from a failure to understand how meaning is conveyed in the Bible or from a failure to apprehend that meaning in an unprejudiced spiritual manner. In Coleridge's words, "If the power of the Spirit from without furnished the text, the grace of the same Spirit from within must supply the comment" (p. 77).

Opposed to strict literal interpretation and recognizing the flexibility of scriptural meaning, Coleridge's hermeneutics as described here have much in common with medieval theological methods whereby passages in the Bible are understood to have a spiritual meaning which can operate on many different levels.[8] For this medieval school of thought— which remained influential into the nineteenth century— the literal sense of a scriptural passage is only one of its possible meanings. There is in addition a typical sense, a *sensus plenior* ("fuller sense" or "sense of the Spirit"), and a so-called accommodated sense.[9] For Coleridge all these levels communicate vital truths: the literal sense of a passage is a necessary safeguard against arbitrary interpretation; the typical sense (in which, for instance, Jonah prefigures Christ) reveals God's providential plan throughout history; the *sensus plenior* is the profound spiritual meaning that is the underpinning of the whole Bible and that has priority over any literal discrepancies; and the accommodated sense is just that—an accommodation of the moral significance of the Scriptures to another purpose, an application of the biblical text to another meaning which the scriptural passage only suggests. Each of these meanings is important to Coleridge's argument in *Confessions of an Inquiring Spirit*, but for my purposes the last level of interpretation is the most significant, since it implies a hermeneutical process in which one text can be translated or *literally* replaced by another text. Coleridge's considerable sympathy for this accommodated sense, moreover, is evident in an 1833 notebook entry in which he speaks of "a justifiable *accommodation* of the Texts of Scripture . . . as expressing the thoughts which the words were fitted to suggest . . . but which, *if* truths & truths of vital interest and import, it may be no presumption to believe, under *this* condition, to have been comprized in the intention of that Holy Spirit, present no less tho' with less manifestation of Power" than the literal sense.[10] Without losing the spirit of a sacred text, in other words, the understanding of it can be to a certain extent relative and depend on who accommodates its meaning and how he accommodates it. Divine reason, the "infallible Intelligence," can manifest itself in several different languages (*Confessions*, p. 14). An uneducated man, for example, can understand or accommodate it his own way, translating it into his own terms, without sacrificing the spiritual truth that is the core of its meaning. Anyone "may study the master-works of our elder divines with safety and advantage, if they will accustom themselves to translate the theological terms into moral equivalents; saying to themselves—This may not be all that is meant, but this is meant, and it is that portion of the meaning, which belongs to me in the present stage of my progress."[11]

In a similar fashion this process can be applied to the interpretation of literature. True, even great works of literature are not the Bible. Yet the truth they can communicate is of the same kind, and the reader can thus benefit from similar methods of exegesis. Works like Aeschylus's *Prometheus*, after all, are holy texts of one sort, and, as one passage already quoted indicates, at least Milton, Shakespeare, Dante, and Homer offer spiritual visions that are comparable with those of the Bible. Further, Coleridge himself suggests that the hermeneutical practices that he urges for scriptural reading can be used in other more profane readings when, equating the two, he demands "for the Bible only the justice which you grant to other proved and acknowledged benefactors of mankind" (*Confessions*, p. 55). Likewise, as part of his argument against literal interpretation of the scriptures, Coleridge notes that the doctrine of infallible communication would naturally be "senseless and self-confuting" to those common-sensical readers who knew enough to "take up the Bible as they do other books, and apply to it the same rules of interpretation" used in reading literature (p. 24). John Tulloch is thus right in emphasizing in 1885 that to Coleridge "belongs the honour of having first plainly and boldly announced that the Scriptures were to be read and studied, like any other literature."[12] But the corollary is equally important or perhaps even more important if we are to appreciate Coleridge's late literary criticism: that is, since the Scriptures and great literature are similar enough to be read the same way, the interpretation of literature should also be allowed the scope of accommodating meaning in terms of other meanings, other languages, and other texts, just like biblical exegesis. Indeed, later in the century, the use of a biblical methodology for literary criticism would be more common, yet an overlooked area of Coleridge's continuing influence on modern literary criticism is his very early application of this methodology to literature. Used in Coleridge's last years, in his *Prometheus* lecture and in much of his marginalia, this process certainly results in some peculiar literary criticism. But this criticism is the product of a sound hermeneutical procedure, directly related to scriptural accommodation, and differing only in that the accommodation is now reversed. Whereas in theological reading *accommodation* usually refers to the understanding of a biblical passage in terms of some action or situation from daily life, after 1820 Coleridge reversed the practice and accommodated literary texts to a theological text. This of course should not be at all surprising, since accommodation is a method for making a text meaningful. Coleridge worked obsessively in these final years to make most everything, especially literature, meaningful in theological terms. To reiterate, "The more tranquilly an inquirer takes up the Bible as he would any other body of writings, the livelier and steadier will be his impressions of its superiority to all other books, till at length all other books and all other knowledge will be valuable in his eyes in proportion as they help him to better understand his Bible" (*Confessions*, p. 84).

Coleridge's essay "On the *Prometheus* of Aeschylus," along with the other literature he read during this period of his life, is therefore the natural product of a hermeneutical method in which a theological discourse completely usurps the work itself in an effort to bring that work's theological significance fully to light. The criticism accommodates the literature to a different language, a new text. Though it is not actually biblical discourse, it is most definitely a theological discourse, with the theological connotations found most prominently in *Church and State* and *Aids to Reflection*. In these two works, two major topics appear, the relationship between Christianity and the acting political government, and the history of Christianity in relation to all history (particularly Hebrew and Greek). The language, terms, and models[13] that Coleridge uses to discuss these topics become the primary codes with which he accommodates the literary texts he interprets during these last years. Faith, Coleridge writes, "must be a light, a form of knowing, a beholding of truth,"[14] and the language of faith in these two prose works becomes a way of knowing Aeschylus's *Prometheus* and many other novels, poems, and plays.

ALTHOUGH AESCHYLUS'S *Prometheus*, as a kind of holy text in its own right, is particularly amenable to this type of accommodation, it is only the most complete and transparent example of Coleridge's critical method in these final years. Much of his other literary criticism and annotations at this time follow the same pattern of accommodation and in a more muted fashion employ terms with special theological connotations as interpretive keys for literature, thus demonstrating Coleridge's complete commitment to this hermeneutical method. To be sure, the other works Coleridge reads and comments on during this period are also extremely responsive to his critical method, since like *Prometheus* they often have rather explicit religious subjects (*Pilgrim's Progress* or *Robinson Crusoe*, for example). But then the choice and selection of material is a frequently ignored critical maneuver in itself; it is the topical significance that he gives these works that makes his literary criticism something other than mere explication. The *Arabian Nights*, for instance, naturally provides good material for Coleridge's discussion of theology and the mythic representation of God's plan. But it is his theological vocabulary, with its special meanings, that distinguishes his comments on that work. Whereas in his early years the supernatural in literature has important political implications, and after 1800 the supernatural in literature is meaningful mostly in terms of a psychology of reader response, during the last years Coleridge is mainly interested in the archetypal meaning of supernatural beings, namely, their meaning in terms of the theological model which he describes in many of his religious prose works of this period and in which power, will, and reason are continually in dynamic tension. Hence many of the supernatural creatures in Asiatic tales and the *Arabian Nights* exemplify, like Jove in *Prometheus*, "the idea of power in the will" (*Criticism*, p. 193). And next to a passage in *Robinson Crusoe* about "the stir people make in the world about ghosts and apparitions," Coleridge turns his thoughts from the supernatural to the religious spirit in all human beings, their divine reason: "I cannot conceive a better definition of Body than Spirit appearing, or of a *flesh and blood man* than a rational spirit apparent" (*Criticism*, p. 298).

One of the more prominent theological issues that entered his reading of *Prometheus* and other literary works at this time is the function of the will in both its divine and human forms. Certainly one of the most important powers in Coleridge's theology, the will means something quite different in the 1820s from its meaning in his earlier years. The moral significance of the word is doubtless always present, but in the middle years the psychological implications of the will almost invariably dwarf its power as an instrument of religion. In Coleridge's *Aids to Reflection*, however, the will is almost exclusively an archetypal moral power, acting in conjunction with the conscience and reason to direct men and women to actions that are harmonious with the will of God. Sacrificing some of the psychological niceties, Coleridge thus asserts more strongly than ever the central position of the will in his theology and morality. Moreover, his literary criticism continues to enforce these theological meanings of the word, often aggressively battling the primary text in order to make his own meaning clear. Thus, a single passage in *Pilgrim's Progress*—"I left off to watch and be sober; I laid the reins upon the neck of my lusts"—generates a short disquisition on Coleridge's conception of the will which could have appeared in *Aids to Reflection* or "Essay on Faith." "This single paragraph proves . . . that in Bunyan's judgment there must be at least a negative co-operation of the will of man with the divine grace, an energy of non-resistance to the workings of the Holy Spirit. But the error of the Calvinists is, that they divide the regenerate will in man from the will of God, instead of including it." [15] Some years earlier, writing on Milton's poems, Coleridge anticipates this remark, and indicates how his notion of the will is crucial to an understanding of man's original sin, a sin always originating in the human will's decision to stray from God's will. The Calvinists are again his foil: "The Calvinists took away all human will. Milton asserted the will, but declared for the enslavement of the will out of an act of will itself" (*Criticism*, p. 163). Although we have fallen, we can still redeem ourselves by responding to our conscience, which is the appendage of our reason and the chief aid of will. If we fail to heed the system of checks and balances, though, the consequences are great; think of *Robinson Crusoe*, where Seignor Atkins, "rebelling against his conscience . . . becomes a slave of his own furious will" (p. 299).

Like this loaded term *will*, there are additional theological terms that appear regularly in Coleridge's literary criticism during these years, although many are inconspicuous because their force and importance lies primarily in Coleridge's theological writings. A rather lengthy attack on Defoe's reference to the devil in *Robinson Crusoe*, for instance, can only seem whimsical and odd unless one knows that Coleridge held the individual will responsible for evil and that the devil is a mere fiction (*Criticism*, pp. 297–98). Similarly, when Coleridge focuses on Robinson Crusoe's awareness of God's miraculous providence, his sensitivity and response to the passage is mostly a product of his theological work and hence tightly bound up with his ideas about history, revealed religion, and his theological model. His marginalia reads: "To make men feel the truth of this once characteristic object of the miracles worked by Moses—the providence miraculous, the miracles providential" (p. 294). But only in *Confessions of an Inquiring Spirit* can the reader discover the full context and theological argument for these miracles providential: "As all Power manifests itself in the harmony of correspondent Opposites, each supposing and supporting the other," Coleridge says here, "so has Religion its objective, or historic and ecclesiastical pole, and its subjective, or spiritual and individual pole. In the miracles and miraculous parts of religion—both in the first communication of divine truths, and in the promulgation of the truths thus communicated—we have the union of the two, that is, the subjective and supernatural displayed objectively—outwardly and phenomenally—as subjective and supernatural" (*Confessions*, pp. 91–92).[16] Finally, there is the marginal note on a line in Scott's *Old Mortality* where, after Scott notes the resistance of the Covenanters "in the cause of civil and religious liberty," Coleridge expands freely on this single line in order to propound his own ideas on intolerance: "Alas! A liberty which in the first moment in which it asserted itself became intolerance, and an exclusion of all liberty in others! But the Scottish Covenanters are not chargeable with this inconsistence. It was not liberty they desired; but truth, which they believe themselves to assert. Now *truth* can be but one. It is in its very essence *exclusive*. It is man's blindness to his own fallibility and the lust of sway which pervert this exclusiveness into *intolerance* and persecution" (*Criticism*, p. 325). The prolixity of this comment however is far less puzzling if the reader realizes it was written under the pressure of the Catholic Emancipation Bill and while Coleridge himself was trying to define tolerance and intolerance. For Coleridge the conflict between the ideal of liberty and the security of truth was an extremely topical matter, and scattered throughout his *Aids to Reflection* and *Church and State* are many finely discriminating definitions of tolerance and intolerance. If the commentary overshadows the text in this case, it is because the text only barely touches on an issue whose public and private importance motivated Coleridge to write at least one book on it.

Perhaps the most resonant literary sounding board for Coleridge's theological discussions (other than *Prometheus*) is *Pilgrim's Progress*, a work that has so much in common with Coleridge's own views that it translates neatly and easily into Coleridge's theology. Indeed, in 1830 Coleridge goes so far as to compare Bunyan's allegory with the Bible. "I know of no book, the Bible excepted," he says, "as above all comparison, which I, according to my judgment and experience, could so safely recommend as teaching and enforcing the whole saving truth according to the mind that was in Christ Jesus, as *Pilgrim's Progress*. It is, in my conviction, incomparably the best *Summa Theologiae Evangelicae* ever produced by a writer not miraculously inspired."[17] *Pilgrim's Progress* becomes in fact a kind of Bible for Coleridge, not a work of literature, and he subsequently applied the same language and nearly the same methods to Bunyan's book that he suggests for the Scriptures. When Bunyan in one line conjoins "Moses' rod with the hammer of the treacherous assassin Jael," Coleridge complains appropriately because the passage offends against the rules for biblical exegesis laid down in *Confessions of an Inquiring Spirit*: it represents "the erroneous preconception that whatever is uttered by a Scripture personage is, in fact, uttered by the infallible Spirit of God."[18]

Yet, using the same code, Coleridge can exonerate Bunyan, since, like the early writers of the sacred Scriptures who made historical errors, Bunyan only errs in the facts, while his spirit and faith are inviolable. "What ought we to infer from this and similar [mistakes in *Pilgrim's Progress*]?" Coleridge asks. He promptly replies "Surely, that the faith in the heart overpowers and renders innocent the errors of the understanding and the delusion of the imagination, and that sincerely pious men purchase, by inconsistency, exemption from the practical consequences of particular errors."[19] In a similar fashion, when Bunyan's persona says that he "walked through the wilderness of this world," Coleridge responds with a long passage that has very little to do with the strictly literary sense of the line, its imagery, or metaphoric strength. Instead, he returns to the model of providential history found in *Aids to Reflection* and (as we shall see) in the *Prometheus* lecture, identifying the Jewish nation's position as a subjective culture as opposed to the objective Greeks, which explains prevalence of the spiritual, subjective sense in their writings. In both the Hebrews' and Bunyan's writings this subjective, symbolic sense determines the meaning: "That in the Apocalypse the wilderness is the symbol of the world, or rather of the wordly life, Bunyan discovered by the instinct of a similar genius. The whole Jewish history, indeed in all its details is so admirably adapted to, and suggestive of, symbolic use, as to justify the belief that the spiritual application, the interior and permanent sense, was in the original intention of the inspiring Spirit, though it might not have been present, as an object of distinct consciousness, to the inspired writers."[20]

Along with Bunyan, Sir Walter Scott also consistently attracts Coleridge's attention in the 1820s. As I have suggested, Coleridge's two major concerns at this period in his life are the correct interpretation of God's providential plan in the Bible and history, and the relation of Church and State as part of that plan. In Bunyan Coleridge discovers primarily a text that he can accommodate to his ideas about interpretation and spiritual meaning; in Scott he finds texts that he can accommodate to his discourse on Church and State. Obviously the two are closely related, just as the model Coleridge uses for his analysis of the Greek and Hebrew cultures serves him in his analysis of the component powers of a Christian nation. But it is in Scott's novels that Coleridge most readily finds congenial remarks and situations that relate to his discussions of Church and State. For, with his profound historical knowledge of the dramatic conflicts over religion and politics, Scott continually provides scenes and incidents that become meaningful for Coleridge almost exclusively in terms of Coleridge's analyses of the Church-and-State issues of his own day.

Central to these analyses is Coleridge's belief that what makes a healthy nation is the balance and interaction of the separate powers within a nation, specifically the powers of permanence and progression (which are the forces interacting with and within the national church). In Coleridge's words, "The two antagonistic powers or opposite interests of the state, under which all other state interests are comprised, are those of PERMANENCE and of PROGRESSION." And the "harmonious balance of the two great correspondent . . . interests of the state, its permanence, and its progression"[21] is neatly linked to the same evolutionary plan that he discerns in the Bible, in modern England, and, finally, in Scott's novels. Unlike the scientific connotations of the polar opposites discussed in *Biographia Literaria*, in Scott's novels the polar opposites therefore refer explicitly to a system of politics and history whose foundation is unquestionably theology. Thus the key to the "wisdom and happiness" found in Scott's entire opus

> consists in this,—that the contest between the loyalists and their opponents can never be *obsolete*, for it is the contest between the two great moving principles of social humanity; religious adherence to the past and the ancient, the desire and admiration of permanence, on the one hand; and the passion for increase of knowledge, for truth, as the offspring of reason—in short, the mighty instincts of *progression* and free agency, on the other. In all subjects of deep and lasting interest, you will detect a struggle between two opposites, two polar forces, both of which are alike necessary to our wellbeing, and necessary each to the continued existence of the other. (*Criticism*, pp. 341–42)

Perhaps the two most indisputable examples of this invasion of *Church and State* into Coleridge's literary criticism, though, are found in some marginal remarks on *The Heart of Midlothian* and *A Legend of Montrose*. On the eve of Catholic emancipation, the Roman Catholic faith, its unique doctrines, and its political threat are of course prominent issues that obtrude rather sharply into his literary criticism. *The Heart of Midlothian* concludes with Lady Staunton's conversion to Catholicism and subsequent retreat to a Catholic convent in order to do penance. But for Coleridge, this dénouement is significant for reasons other than its relation to the main themes of the novel. He writes about this ending: "Perhaps the error of the Romish Church for which the heart pleads most strongly and which mere understanding finds most equitable, is of all others the error that has produced the most evil—fruits most poisonous—the doctrine of purgatory, I mean—as if providence warned us by a proof which all men can understand, how dangerous every addition to revealed truth, however plausible it may appear to our narrow intellect. The heart of man, conscious of its imperfections, is *naturally* too narrow to contain a full faith in the absoluteness of God's love to us in Christ!" (*Criticism*, p. 327). Similarly, commenting on the first chapter of *A Legend of Montrose*, Coleridge draws a parallel between Scott's depiction of Cromwell's struggles with the Scottish Presbyterians and England's present-day problems with the Irish Catholics. In both cases, the difficulties are a result of a failure to appreciate the delicate balance between the national church and other Christian sects: "Cromwell restrained and curbed, but did not *overset*, the Presbyterian Church in Scotland. Had the coalition of the two forms, each modifying the other, been *practicable*, it *would* have been a most desirable event, an irresistable arm of strength to both countries and the solid foundation of their future union as *one* state. That which in an intenser form has rendered the union with Ireland a calamitous mockery, delayed the blessings of union more than a century for Scotland" (p. 328).

THE TEXTS OF SCOTT AND BUNYAN, however, are casual exercises of a method that only appears with its full force in Coleridge's *Prometheus* lecture, where from the outset Coleridge establishes a rather unusual context for his discussion of the play, making it fully obvious that his approach will be unorthodox. "The French *savans* who went to Egypt in the train of Bounaparte [*sic*], Denon, Fourrier, and Dupuis, (it has been asserted), triumphantly vindicated the chronology of Herodotus, on the authority of documents that cannot lie."[22] Thus reads the first sentence. And he continues in this vein for some time without the slightest hint of how it applies to *Prometheus*. His discussion in these opening pages focuses on the religion of the Egyptians and its relation to the history of the Jews. He rarely argues, though, preferring simply to assert findings more carefully proved in other works and finally to conclude that "the religion of Egypt, at the time of the Exodus of the Hebrews, was a pantheism, on the point of passing into that polytheism, of which it afterwards afforded a specimen, gross and distasteful to the polytheists themselves of other nations" (*"Prometheus,"* 2 : 330).

Talking about polytheism and pantheism, Coleridge seems to be drawing nearer to Aeschylus's play, since he is at least in the area of Greek religion at this point. Accordingly he suddenly breaks off and announces his goals for now and later, goals that bring *Prometheus* into view:

> The objects which, on my appointment as Royal Associate of the Royal Society of Literature, I proposed for myself were, 1st. The elucidation of the purpose of the Greek drama, and the relations in which it stood to the mysteries on the one hand, and to the state or sacerdotal religion on the other:—2nd. The connection of the

Greek tragic poets with philosophy as the peculiar off-spring of Greek genius;—3rd. The connection of the Homeric and cyclical poets with the popular religion of the Greeks: and, lastly from all these,—namely, the mysteries, the sacerdotal religion, their philosophy before and after Socrates, the stage, the Homeric poetry and the legendary belief of the people, and from the sources and productive causes in the derivation and confluence of the tribes that finally shaped themselves into a nation of Greeks—to give a juster and more distinct view of this singular people, and the place which they occupied in the history of the world, and the great scheme of divine providence. (2:330)

This abrupt promulgation, with its typically Coleridgean cosmic scope, clearly does not make the essay easier to follow. Yet it does indicate its direction, and begins to suggest why Coleridge introduces so much prefatory material. For Coleridge the early Greek religions also practice a kind of pantheism that is misinterpreted as polytheism. Greek pantheism is not opposed to the Hebrew religion (as Coleridge perceives it) but, like the Egyptian religion, it is in harmony with, though contradistinguished from, the Jewish faith, since both are part of "the great scheme of divine providence" and a monotheistic belief. More importantly, only by understanding how God's plan (Coleridge's version of it, anyway) manifests itself in this period and how it struggles against popular heretical beliefs can one properly appreciate the art of Greeks. Reining in his mammoth proposal, Coleridge therefore proceeds:

The present Essay, however, I devote to the purpose of removing, or at least invalidating, one objection that I may reasonably anticipate, and which may be conveyed in the following question:—What proof have you of the fact of any connection between the Greek drama, and either the mysteries, or the philosophy, of Greece? What proof that it was the office of the tragic poet, under a disguise of the sacerdotal religion, mixed with the legendary or popular belief, to reveal as much of the mysteries interpreted by philosophy, as would counteract the demoralizing effects of the state religion, without compromising the tranquillity of the state itself, or weakening the paramount reverence without which a republic, (such I mean, as the republics of ancient Greece were) could not exist?

I know no better way in which to reply to this objection, than by giving, as my proof and instance, the Prometheus of Aeschylus, accompanied with an exposition of what I believe to be the intention of the poet, and the mythic import of the work. (2:331)

Coleridge claims, in short, that there is a particular model which describes how God has revealed himself through history and in different societies, that this model can be descried at many points in history, and that we see this truth most accurately produced in great works of art, or more specifically, in Aeschylus's *Prometheus*. For Coleridge, this monotheistic providence informs all that is worthwhile in history from its beginning in the Hebrew culture through the Egyptian and Greek societies and its culmination in Christianity. He says

that in whatever has permanent operation on the destinies and intellectual condition of mankind at large,— that in all which has been manifestly employed as a co- agent in the mightiest revolution of the moral world, the propagation of the Gospel, and in the intellectual progress of mankind in the restoration of philosophy,

science, and the ingenious arts—it were irreligious not
to acknowledge the hand of divine providence. The periods, too, join on to each other. The earliest Greeks
took up the religious and lyrical poetry of the Hebrews; and the schools of the prophets were, however
partially and imperfectly, represented by the mysteries
derived through the corrupt channel of the Phoenicians. (2 : 332–33)

Prometheus becomes, then, a dramatic illustration and
flowering of the providential scheme that is the foundation
of Coleridge's version of history: in *Prometheus* the artistic
mythus becomes the divine plan appearing in a concrete historical form. To be sure, Greek art embodies this law differently from Hebrew or Christian art: "This the most vener-
able, and perhaps the most ancient, of Grecian *mythi*, is a
philosopheme, the very same in subject matter with the earliest record of the Hebrews, but most characteristically different in tone and conception;—for the patriarchal religion,
as the antithesis of pantheism, was necessarily personal; and
the doctrines of a faith, the first ground of which and the primary enunciation, is the eternal I AM, must be in part historic and must assume the historic form" (2:335). And this
difference results from their different positions in a linear
history. In the Hebrew religion there is "a *synthesis* of poesy
and philosophy, characteristic of the childhood of nations"
(2:336). "In the Greek we see already the dawn of approaching manhood. The substance, the stuff is philosophy; the
form only is poetry. The Prometheus is a philosophema
. . .—the tree of knowledge of good and evil,—an allegory,
. . . though the noblest and most pregnant of its kind" (2:336).
Significantly, when Coleridge speaks of *Prometheus* as an allegory here, there is none of the condescension with which
he compares allegory to symbol in *Biographia Literaria*. In

these final years the divine law of theology is far more important than the more subtle generic distinctions of earlier years.

This divine law or plan that links the Hebrew, Greek, and Christian cultures and provides the structural foundation for *Prometheus* appears in many of Coleridge's works during the 1820s. In its most abstract form it could be described this way:

	Prothesis	
Thesis	Mesothesis	Antithesis
	Synthesis	

More frequently, however, it appears in its Christian formulation, which is clearly where its greatest significance lies for Coleridge. In *Confessions of an Inquiring Spirit*, Coleridge calls this model the pentad of operative Christianity and attaches a brief explanation:

	Prothesis	
	Christ, the Word	
Thesis	Mesothesis	Antithesis
The Scriptures	The Holy Spirit	The Church
	Synthesis	
	The Preacher	

The Scriptures, the Spirit, and the Church, are co-ordinate; the indispensable conditions and the working causes of the perpetuity, and continued renascence and spiritual life of Christ still militant. (*Confessions*, p. x)

For Coleridge, "this is God's Hand in the World," and in this final Christian form, it is the pinnacle of the divine providential scheme.

Applied to Aeschylus's *Prometheus* this model becomes an interpretive code in the strictest sense of the word; it

COLERIDGE, THEOLOGY, AND LITERARY CRITICISM

truly creates a meaning that derives from the more abstract formulation but which receives its ultimate significance from the Christian formulation Coleridge always has in mind. The easiest part of this formula is certainly Coleridge's explanation of the two main characters in the play, Prometheus and Jove. Jove becomes rather mechanically equated or aligned with the thesis of Coleridge's model, and Prometheus takes the antithetical position. These two poles are also described as law and idea: "Now according to the Greek philosopheme or *mythus*," Coleridge says, "there arose a war, schism, or division, that is, a polarization into *thesis* and *antithesis*. In consequence of this schism . . . the *thesis* becomes *nomos*, or law, and the *antithesis* becomes idea" ("*Prometheus*," 2:343). Ideally functioning in union, idea and law are correlatives, and "the ground work of the Aeschylean *mythus* is laid in the definition of idea and law, as correlatives that mutually interpret each other; an idea, with the adequate power of realizing itself being a law, and a law considered abstractedly from, or in the absence of, the power of manifesting itself in its appropriate product being an idea" (2:348). The relation between the Church as antithesis and the Scriptures as thesis certainly fits this description (especially in light of Coleridge's statements about how the Platonic idea of the Church can be corrupted by power). But, more importantly, the dramatic characters in Aeschylus's play become representatives of these two poles, tragically separated after a prelapsarian union: in *Prometheus* "Jove is the impersonated representation or symbol of the *nomos—Jupiter est quodcunque vides*. He is the *mens agitans molem*, but at the same time, the *molem corpoream et constituens*. . . . Prometheus, in like manner, is the impersonated representative of Idea, or the same power as Jove, but contemplated as independent and not immersed in the product,—a law *minus* the productive energy" (2:350).

Following the hermeneutical method he uses for the Bible, Coleridge then lists four ways of interpreting Jove and ten ways of interpreting Prometheus. These, Coleridge asserts in an uncompromising tone, "are the meaning of the fable" and play (2 : 350), and their sometimes obvious connections with the Christian faith are major determinants in what the play means to Coleridge. Jove, for example, can represent a type of Old Testament "father . . . as sovereign" but also "law in the Pauline sense" (2:348). Conversely, half of Prometheus's possible meanings indicate that he is a kind of Christ, an inference which Coleridge reinforces by describing him in Miltonic or biblical language: Prometheus is "the divine humanity, the human God" who "gave that which, according to the whole analogy of things, should have existed either as pure divinity . . . or was conceded to inferior beings as a *substans in substantatio*." He is the giver becoming the gift, "the gift 'whence the soul receives reason; and reason is her being' (in Milton's words)"; he is knowledge and prophecy, " 'the Word of the Lord in the mouth of the Prophet'"; he is noetic man, knowing nature because he is above nature; and finally Prometheus as Christ is the progenitor of an "Alcides Liberator" (2:352–58).

The meaning of the two characters therefore is at least rhetorically dependent on their being representatives of the thesis and antithesis in Coleridge's model-positions, which in turn receive most of their connotative force from the Christian faith. If the manifestations in the play of the other powers in Coleridge's theological model are less clear, the reason is that Aeschylus's play itself is so barely populated with characters. This does not however prevent Coleridge from implying their presence in the drama, and in fact producing their presence by keeping close to his theological model and terminology. Of these other powers the prothesis would naturally be the power most difficult, if not impossible, to locate in the play. Yet, as I have been indicating, Coleridge is less interested in rephrasing meaning than in making a meaning that "should" be there—even if it is not textually evident. He is less interested in what is written in the first text than what he can write in the second text.

Thus, midway through the essay, he introduces into his discussion of the Prometheus myth "the unevolved, unproduced, *prothesis*," of which Prometheus and Jove "are the *thesis* and *antithesis*" (2:342). Coleridge goes to great lengths to explain this power, and once again his explanation gains most of its force and much of its significance from a comparison of Aeschylus's myth with the prothesis of the Judeo-Christian and Phoenician religions. "The Hebrew wisdom," Coleridge argues, "imperatively asserts an unbeginning creative One, who neither became the world; nor is the world eternally; nor made the world out of himself by emanation, or evolution;—but who willed it and it was! . . . and this chaos, the eternal will . . . enabled to become a world" (2: 340). The Phoenicians, on the other hand, confuse the natural product with its supernatural beginning: "With the Phoenician sages the cosmogony was their theogony and *vice versa*. Hence, too flowed their theurgic rites, their magic, their worship" (2 : 339–40). The prothesis "preserved for us in the Aeschylean Prometheus," however, "stands midway betwixt both, yet is distinct in kind from either" the Hebrew or Phoenician myth. "With the Hebrew or purer Semitic, it assumes . . . an indeterminate *Elohim*, antecedent to the matter of the world. . . . In this point, likewise, the Greek accorded with the Semitic, and differed from the Phoenician—that it held the antecedent . . . to be supersensuous and divine. But on the other hand it coincides with the Phoenician in considering this antecedent ground of corporeal matter . . . not so properly the cause of the latter, as the occasion and still continuing substance. . . . The corporeal was supposed coessential with the antecedent of its corporeity" (2:340–41).

Not concretely present in the play, Coleridge's long delineation here of Aeschylus's prothesis in terms of the Judeo-

Christian belief is "the key to the whole cypher of the Aeschylean mythology" (2:342). Strict literary criticism this analysis certainly is not: "All this will seem strange and obscure at first reading,—perhaps fantastic," Coleridge admits, "but it will only seem so" to the unpenetrating eye, since this highly abstract investigation is crucial to a proper understanding of the play. Accordingly Coleridge sums up the Greek prothesis with an explication that depends even more explicitly on Judeo-Christian references. He writes: "First, what Moses appropriated to the chaos itself, . . . the containing [proposition] of the *thesis* and *antithesis*;—this the Greek placed anterior to the chaos; . . . Secondly, what Moses establishes, not merely as transcendent *Monas*, but as an individual [oneness] likewise; this the Greek took as a harmony" (2:342). Further, it is from the struggle inherent within the Greek prothesis that the schism between thesis and antithesis, idea and law, arises. As opposed to the Hebrew *mythus* in which the schism is a product of the prothesis's will, this break or division is an inevitable part of the beginning. Since this break and the repercussions from it are the central topics of *Prometheus*, moreover, the distinctions that Coleridge makes here are of paramount importance in his understanding of what that play means.

In a similar manner, Coleridge's points about the mesothesis in Aeschylus's play receive most of their significance from the implied contrast he sets up between the Christian mesothesis and the language he uses to discuss that Christian power. In its Christian form the mesothesis is the Holy Spirit, who acts as a liaison between the law and the idea, thus representing the conjunction which religion must always strive for. In terms of the individual, the grace of the Holy Spirit represents faith or the union of will and reason. In Aeschylus's *Prometheus*, however, will remains separate from reason, just as law opposes idea; the powerful will, the person of Jove, is in fact at war with powerless reason—Prometheus—in this play. Yet there is a possible reconciler of the two gods in *Prometheus*: Hermes, who acts as a bridge or link to bring the two together, and who, as Coleridge describes him in his lecture, becomes a tragic parody of the Christian Holy Spirit. Coleridge observes of Prometheus that many "kindred deities come to him, some to soothe, to condole; others to give weak, yet friendly counsels of submission; others to tempt, or insult. The most prominent of the latter, and the most odious to the imprisoned and insulated *Nous*, is Hermes, the impersonation of interest, . . . as interest or motives intervening between the reason and its immediate self-determinations. . . . But, primarily, the Hermes is the symbol of interest. He is the messenger, the inter-nuncio, in the low but expressive phrase, the go-between, to beguile or insult" (2 : 355 – 56). Hermes attempts to seduce Prometheus into surrendering his rational powers to the sensual world. He is consequently a kind of carnal Holy Spirit, a Satanic spirit, who attempts to pervert the divine idea by appealing to self-interest. Coleridge therefore describes him with the same language he uses to depict the Catholic church in his other writings; like the Catholic church, which has been seduced away from the divine idea of the Church, Hermes represents "the eloquence of cupidity, the cajolement of power regnant; and in a larger sense, custom, the irrational in language, the fluent" (2 : 356). In brief, as Hermes is a venal and thus fallen Holy Spirit, the Catholic church is a venal and fallen Prometheus.

In addition to this schematic interpretation of Hermes, the Christian mesothesis or Holy Spirit bears on *Prometheus* and other Greek literature in yet another way, which is also clearly related to the disjunction dramatized in Aeschylus's play. As the potentially perfect conjunction of will and reason, the Christian Holy Spirit, Coleridge claims, attains its most perfect form in Christ, the original prothesis. Christ, then, represents the highest manifestation of individuality as the union of individual reason with the divine will. In his *Aids to Reflection*, Coleridge explains this most perfect kind of individuality, which is a gift of the Holy Spirit, as a state in which the individual's will and reason become one with the divine will and law, in which "the will constitutes the law," thus removing "the commanding, binding, and menacing character which belongs to a law, acting as a master or sovereign" like Jove.[23] As a rational though fallen being, the Christian can reach this state of harmony through the grace of the Holy Spirit. For the fallen, unchristian Prometheus, however, the conflict remains unresolved: individuality has not been perfected because the evolution of the individual has not been completed. Again, God's providential historical plan, according to which the Hebrew and Greek cultures are partial and incomplete stages in the historical development of the perfect individual, Christ and the Christian, explains this conflict: whereas the Hebrew culture embodies a predominance of will, the Greek embodies a predominance of reason. Only in the personal and historical confluence of the two does true individuality blossom. Discussing how the Greek and Hebrew cultures prepared for Christ's coming, Coleridge notes that "at length the two great component parts of our nature, in the unity of which all its excellency and all its hopes depend, namely that of will in the one, as the higher and more especially godlike, and the reason in the other, as the compeer but yet second to that will, were to unite and to prepare for the reception of its Redeemer."[24] Or, in Owen Barfield's words, "It was in the polarity between the two cultures that progress—that is, the evolution of the individual—above all resided; in the polarity and in the varying predominances by which polarity is characterized. Thus, in point of the man } { God relation, experience of the will aspect of reason was predominant in the Hebrew mind; experience of the reason aspect [of reason] in the Greek."[25] In "all that makes Greece Greece to us," Coleridge says, "that power was predetermined by Almighty Providence to gradually evolve all that could be evolved out of corrupt nature by its own reason; while on the opposite ground there was a nation bred up by inspiration in a childlike form, in obedience and in the exercise of the will."[26] Thus, just as his separation from will and law is what makes the Greek Prometheus subjectively weak, saps him of the strength of individuality, and binds him to the rock, this same imperfect individuality and lack of subjectivity suffuses all Greek literature. The consequent imbalance explains why "Prometheus, in the old mythus, and for the most part in Aeschylus, is the Redeemer and the Devil jumbled together."[27] And in 1832 Coleridge uses the same historical-theological model to make one of the most interesting stylistic comments on Greek literature: "The want of adverbs in the Iliad is very characteristic. With more adverbs there would have been some subjectivity, or subjectivity would have made them. The Greeks were just then on the verge of the bursting forth of individuality."[28]

As a rather malleable grid upon which Coleridge plots his theological model, Aeschylus's *Prometheus* derives its significance, as we have seen, primarily from the model and not the play: Coleridge's theological discourse, that is, makes the meaning of the play by controlling the elements of the play in a certain way and at least implying (often directly stating) a comparison or contrast with the Judeo-Christian manifestations of the same powers as he describes them in *Aids to Reflection* and other theological documents. (The fifth power on the grid, the synthesis, would be the play itself.)

But *Prometheus* also draws on the other part of the theological discourse that figures so importantly in Coleridge's life at this time. Very closely related to his model of the history of Christianity, this other side of his theology is presented most cogently in *Church and State*, in which he deals with the role of the Christian church within a political system. Granted the concerns and language of this discourse are not so central to his analysis of *Prometheus*, yet nonetheless they appear, sometimes obtrusively, to direct the meaning of the play. Hermes, as we have seen, represents a self-interest and sensuality that Coleridge regularly associates with the Catholic church. The identification of the two is quite logical and meaningful when one realizes that the occasion of *Church and State* is the heated debates over the Catholic Emancipation Acts, acts that Coleridge was hardly enthusiastic about. More significantly, the tension and interaction which Coleridge claims is the ideal relation of Church and State becomes for him the key to the genesis of Aeschylus's entire play. Writing to James Gillman he explains the relationship of Church and State with the same pentadic model that serves him throughout these years, thus illustrating how the theology overshadows the politics:

	Prothesis Nation	
Thesis State	*Mesothesis* The Press	*Antithesis* The Church
	Synthesis The Crown[29]	

Following this model, Coleridge argues for the interdependence and separation of the powers of Church and State, so that they may productively and correctively interact in order to create a more cultivated, religious, and secure nation. Being loyal to a foreign head of state, the Catholic church would naturally be disqualified as an active member of this organization. Moreover, a church whose priorities were first with the state would relinquish its freedom and so destroy the healthy dialectic within the nation.

This last problem is what plagued the Greek nation during Aeschylus's life, and according to Coleridge it helps explain the creative impetus behind the whole play. Early in his lectures Coleridge lists as one of his projects "the elucidation of the purpose of the Greek drama, and the relations in which it stood to the mysteries on the one hand, and to the state or sacerdotal religion on the other" ("*Prometheus*," 2:330). Later he focuses this problem when he predicates that *Prometheus* is Aeschylus's disguised attempt to reestablish the proper religion and its proper relation to the state—reestablish, in other words, Coleridge's holy model: *Prometheus* "under the disguise of the sacerdotal religion, mixed with the legendary or popular belief" reveals "as much of the mysteries as interpreted by philosophy, as would counteract the demoralizing effects of the state religion, without compromising the tranquillity of the state itself, or weakening that paramount reverence, without which a republic, (such I mean, as the republics of ancient Greece were) could not exist" (2:331). Becoming more conservative in his views, Coleridge makes a special point of distinguishing the conservative republic of Greece from the revolutionary republics springing up in his own day. He insists on his language and his meanings here, just as he insists on his models and evaluations throughout *Prometheus*. In this case it is specifically his concept of the Christian state that produces the meaning. But throughout the essay his theological discourse nearly transforms the play as his model translates it: *Prometheus* exemplifies his theological model of the fall of man; it manifests God's providential use of that model through history; and it is created out of Aeschylus's need to reestablish that model in the larger political network of religion.

Indeed, Coleridge's commentaries on Aeschylus's *Prometheus* and the other works he read at this period of his life stretch literary criticism to its limits. To argue that it is truly literary criticism in fact would raise a great many eyebrows, unless the argument begins by noting that all criticism is a kind of accommodation to some extent and that in these years Coleridge's is simply accommodation in its freest form. Indeed, when Coleridge remains near the primary text in the 1820s his remarks resemble much conventional criticism. His accommodations seem then to be the finer discriminations or subtle translations of a single concept that are admired in his acute textual analyses of Wordsworth's poems in *Biographia Literaria*.[30] More frequently, however, when Coleridge's critical accommodations of drama or poetry leave the primary text far behind, the literary criticism becomes quite difficult to recognize and far more difficult to defend. In the last examples I have given, the primary text becomes a palimpsest whose original message seems important only as the barest foundation for the later commentary. The margins are never quite large enough for Coleridge in these years; their boundaries are continually pushed back until the material between them seems mostly insignificant. In each of my examples the pressure that once came from disciplines like politics or science and that informed Coleridge's literary language and judgments at other times now comes from theology with such a powerful authority that the interaction and meeting of two texts, which describes all criticism, becomes instead a complete conquest by the theological text. The spiritual meaning of theology, in short, takes precedence over the lesser spiritual meaning of literature. Moreover, readers that claim this is not literary criticism are using a definition of *literary* that is not necessarily accurate. For, above all else, literary criticism is a process, a confrontation of two minds through the meeting of two texts. In this meeting one usually expects more courtesy toward the primary text than Coleridge usually shows in these last years. But Coleridge's lack of deference is something other than crudity or rudeness; if he manhandles his material at times he clearly does not lack respect for *Prometheus* or the works of Scott, but rather feels a passion for the theological truths and meanings that in his final days are overwhelmingly more important than psychological niceties, political ethics, or problems of organic form. Earlier in his career Coleridge may have felt it crucial to create meaning for literature in the language of mankind and its business; in his last years Coleridge understandably felt that literature should bring mankind back to the language of God.

CONCLUSION
The Tangential Critic

Accustom yourself to reflect on the words you use,
hear, or read, their birth, derivation and history.
For if words are not things, they are living powers,
by which the things of most importance to
mankind are actuated, combined, and humanized.

COLERIDGE,
Aids to Reflection

ABOVE ALL ELSE, MY ARGUMENT here has tried to demonstrate that Coleridge was a historical man who responded to pertinent issues in a concretely historical manner. More than simply an idealist, Coleridge was a careful literary critic whose concept of that function was, in William Rueckert's words, "to study and speak about literature (any literature) and/or literary criticism in the language and terminology of his own time, for his own time. A critic may draw some of his terms from a conceptual model more than two thousand years old, . . . but he must still speak in the language of his own time, to issues of his own time, for his own time, and about his own time."[1] Besides perceiving the unity of history and the oneness of life, Coleridge also recognized that within this unity specific issues gain prominence, that periods of time can be distinguished and defined in their particularity, and that the difference between types of knowledge and types of language has crucial, practical repercussions in the quality of life. This is the historical sense and intellectual breadth that Hazlitt hailed in 1825 as the energy and nobility of Coleridge's "tangential" mind, a mind able to participate in a nearly infinite variety of knowledges. In Hazlitt's words, "There is no subject on which he has not touched, none on which he has rested. With an understanding, fertile, subtle, expansive . . . he lends himself to all impressions alike; he gives up his mind and liberty of thought to none. He is a general lover of art and science, and wedded to no one in particular."[2] Actuating this mobility and range as he saw fit, Coleridge drew on this extraordinary bank of knowledge as the times demanded; it was the historical exigencies, the particular needs of the day, that naturally told Coleridge what to speak to. If his monistic foundation was ever present, if he was always assimilating the languages of his past into his present, nonetheless it was the issues of the historical present that called out most strongly to Coleridge and that he was quick to answer in their own idiom.

In the same way, literature and art may represent timeless forces and truths, but criticism and its langauges are very much of the temporal domain. For Coleridge, one may read eternity in a poem, but one can explain that poem only to a historical present. The languages of criticism, like all discursive languages, are the languages of history, and these languages should accordingly answer the demands of history. Thus, when the language of politics or the language of science rises in time to challenge those absolute, humanistic truths of which poetry is the guardian, criticism should reply to that language in its own tongue.

In this confrontation, both realms are affected; both texts profit. The language of science, for example, should be affected as much as the meaning of poetry when the two merge in the text of the *Biographia Literaria*. And it is in this sense that the words of a good critic are "living powers, by which the things of most importance to mankind are actuated, combined, and humanized."[3]

As Coleridge practiced it, then, literary criticism becomes a liaison between poetry and practical, historical matters. The critic is the translator of poetic spirituality into practical humanity. As the definer of the poem he is the redefiner of those historical forms—words—in terms of those timeless, speechless truths of the spirit. Creatively deconstructing what the poet creatively constructs, he is the producer of many meanings as he transports the poem's significance outside its own boundaries into the flux of history.

Clearly Coleridge felt poetry's profound truths and spoke

fluently within its borders. He felt them so deeply, in fact, that throughout his life he struggled indefatigably to express those truths in the languages of all other people. He read poetry with as much imagination and energy as was expended in its writing. For him, the margins were to be as full as the text itself, and his task as a reader-critic was to carry poetry's message into the many meanings of the margins.

Notes

Introduction

1. Jonathan Culler, *Structuralist Poetics* (Ithaca, N.Y.: Cornell University Press, 1975), pp. 134, 137.

2. Jonathan Culler, "Literary History, Allegory, and Semiology," *New Literary History* 7 (1976): 260.

3. Jacques Derrida, "Structure, Sign, and Play in the Discourse of the Human Sciences," in *The Structuralist Controversy: The Languages of Criticism and the Sciences of Man*, ed. Richard Macksey and Eugenio Donato (Baltimore, Md.: Johns Hopkins Press, 1970), p. 260; Roland Barthes, *S/Z* (New York: Hill and Wang, 1974), p. 9.

4. S. T. Coleridge, *Miscellaneous Criticism*, ed. T. M. Raysor (Cambridge: Harvard University Press, 1936), p. 343.

CHAPTER ONE
Coleridge, the Reader:
Language in a Combustible Mind

1. S. T. Coleridge, *On the Constitution of the Church and State*, ed. John Colmer (London: Routledge and Kegan Paul, 1976), p. 134.

2. S. T. Coleridge, *The Friend*, ed. Barbara E. Rooke (London: Routledge and Kegan Paul, 1969), 1:52. In this chapter, further references are found in the text. Since Rooke was unable to trace the source of this passage, it is of course conceivable that Coleridge himself might be the author.

3. Phillipe Sollers, *Logiques* (Paris: Seuil, 1968), pp. 237–38.

4. S. T. Coleridge, *Shakespearean Criticism*, ed. T. M. Raysor (London: Dent and Sons, 1960), 2:39.

5. S. T. Coleridge, *Biographia Literaria*, ed. J. Shawcross (London: Oxford University Press, 1907), 1:34n. In this chapter, further references are found in the text.

6. Wolfgang Iser, "The Reading Process: A Phenomenological Approach," in *New Directions in Literary History*, ed. Ralph Cohen (Baltimore: Johns Hopkins University Press, 1974), p. 130. The article originally appeared in *New Literary History*.

7. Owen Barfield, *What Coleridge Thought* (Middletown, Conn.: Wesleyan University Press, 1971), p. 97.

8. Ibid., p. 101.

9. S. T. Coleridge, *Aids to Reflection*, ed. Henry Nelson Coleridge (New York: William Gowans, 1863), pp. 16–17.

10. S. T. Coleridge, *Lay Sermons*, ed. R. J. White (London: Routledge and Kegan Paul, 1972), p. 59.

11. Barfield, *What Coleridge Thought*, p. 96.

12. Cited in Richard Haven, *Patterns of Consciousness* (Amherst: University of Massachusetts Press, 1969), p. 14.

13. Coleridge, *Shakespearean Criticism*, 1:103–4.

14. *The Complete Poetical Works of Samuel Taylor Coleridge*, ed. Ernest Hartley Coleridge (London: Oxford University Press, 1912), 1:407, 408.

15. *The Complete Works of Samuel Taylor Coleridge*, ed. W. G. T. Shedd (New York: Harper Brothers, 1858), 5:286. This fragment is from a note on Luther's *Table Talk*.

16. Marginalia published in Robert Southey, *The Life of Wesley* (London: Oxford University Press, 1925), 2:58–59n.

17. Coleridge, *Aids to Reflection*, p. 174.

18. Cited in Barfield, *What Coleridge Thought*, p. 223 (n. 30). Note in J. F. Blumenbach, *Über die natürlichen Verschiedenheiten*.

19. Barfield, *What Coleridge Thought*, p. 99.

20. Coleridge, *Aids to Reflection*, p. 173.

21. George Steiner, *After Babel* (London: Oxford University Press, 1975), p. 79; see particularly J. Isaacs, "Coleridge's Critical Terminology," *Essays and Studies* 21 (1936): 86–105; Owen Barfield, "Coleridge's Enjoyment of Words," in *Coleridge's Variety*, ed. John Beer (Pittsburgh: University of Pittsburgh Press, 1975), pp. 204–19; and also Barfield's *What Coleridge Thought*.

22. *Collected Letters of Samuel Taylor Coleridge*, ed. E. L. Griggs, 6 vols. (London: Oxford University Press, 1956–71), 1:625–26.

23. Quoted from an unpublished manuscript in *Inquiring Spirit:*

A New Presentation of Coleridge from His Published and Unpublished Prose Writings, ed. Kathleen Coburn (New York: Minerva Press, 1951), pp. 101–2.

24. Coleridge, "On the Principles of Genial Criticism," in *Biographia*, 2:226.

25. Barfield, "Coleridge's Enjoyment of Words," p. 217.

26. *S. T. Coleridge's Treatise on Method*, ed. Alice D. Snyder (London: Constable and Co., 1934), p. 6.

27. Barfield, "Coleridge's Enjoyment of Words," p. 212.

28. Cited in Coleridge, *Friend*, 1:474 (n. 1). It appears in a MS fragment.

29. S. T. Coleridge, "Hints towards a More Comprehensive Theory of Life," in *Miscellanies, Aesthetic and Literary*, ed. T. Ashe (London: G. Bell, 1911), p. 585; idem, *Letters*, 1:625–26.

30. Barfield, "Coleridge's Enjoyment of Words," p. 212.

31. *The Notebooks of Samuel Taylor Coleridge*, ed. Kathleen Coburn (New York: Pantheon Books, 1957), vol. 1, no. 1387.

32. Quoted in Barfield, *What Coleridge Thought*, p. 204 (n. 29), from a note on the flyleaf of Tennemann's *Geschichte der Philosophie*, vol. 7.

33. Haven, *Patterns of Consciousness*, p. 154.

34. Coleridge, *Notebooks*, vol. 1, no. 1016.

35. Ibid., no. 383.

36. Coleridge, *Friend*, 1:176; and idem, *Aids to Reflection*, p. 178.

37. George Steiner, "Whorf, Chomsky, and the Student of Literature," *New Literary History* 4 (1972): 16.

38. S. T. Coleridge, *Lectures 1795 on Politics and Religion*, ed. Lewis Patton and Peter Mann (London: Routledge and Kegan Paul, 1971), p. 141.

39. S. T. Coleridge, *The Philosophical Lectures*, ed. Kathleen Coburn (New York: Philosophical Library, 1949), p. 168.

40. Coleridge, *Letters*, 4:688.

41. Coleridge, *Table Talk*, 27 Dec. 1831.

42. Coleridge, *Letters*, 5:168.

43. Sollers, *Logiques*, p. 220.

44. M. H. Abrams, *The Mirror and the Lamp* (London: Oxford University Press, 1953), p. 31.

45. Steiner, *After Babel*, p. 47.

46. Roman Jakobson, "On Linguistic Aspects of Translation," in *Selected Writings* (The Hague: Mouton, 1971), 2:266.

CHAPTER TWO
The Politics of Rhetoric
in Coleridge's Early Criticism

1. Coleridge, *Letters*, 4:713.

2. The two standard examinations of Coleridge's politics are John Colmer's *Coleridge: Critic of Society* (London: Oxford University Press, 1959) and Carl Woodring's *Politics in the Poetry of Coleridge* (Madison: University of Wisconsin Press, 1961). A third good treatment is Alfred Cobban's chapter on Coleridge's political career in *Edmund Burke and the Revolt against the Eighteenth Century* (Northampton: John Dickens and Co., 1929). More recently, there is David Erdman's introduction to *Essays on His Times*, ed. David Erdman (Princeton, N.J.: Princeton University Press, 1978).

3. Coleridge, *Biographia*, 1:121.

4. Cobban, *Edmund Burke*, p. 166.

5. Coleridge, *Letters*, 1:222.

6. Coleridge, *Lectures 1795*, p. lvii. In this chapter, further references are found in the text.

7. Coleridge, *Complete Poetical Works*, 1:106–8.

8. Coleridge, *Letters*, 1:277.

9. See Woodring's *Politics*.

10. Coleridge, *Notebooks*, vol. 1, no. 87. In this chapter, further references are found in the text.

11. S. T. Coleridge, *The Watchman*, ed. Lewis Patton (London: Routledge and Kegan Paul, 1970), pp. 139–40. In this chapter, further references are found in the text.

12. Coleridge, *Complete Poetical Works*, 1:115.

13. The substantial changes and additions that Coleridge made in these notes between the editions of 1796 and 1797 suggests an increasing concern with the political significance of the poetry.

14. Coleridge, *Table Talk*, 7 May 1830.

15. Colmer, *Coleridge*, p. 24.

16. Coleridge, *Essays on His Times*, 1:114.

17. Ibid., p. 223.

18. Colmer, *Coleridge*, p. 177.

19. Coleridge, *Letters*, 1:248.

20. Colmer, *Coleridge*, p. 9.

21. Coleridge, *Criticism*, p. 163.

22. Benjamin T. Sankey, "Coleridge on Milton's Satan," *Philological Quarterly* 41 (1962): 505.

23. Coleridge, *Complete Poetical Works*, 2:1136.

24. Ibid.

25. Coleridge, *Letters*, 1:146.

26. *The British Critic*, vol. 554. Quoted in Coburn's note to Coleridge's text in *Notebooks*, vol. 1, no. 48.

27. Coleridge, *Complete Poems*, 2:1145.

28. Coleridge, *Letters*, 1:164.

29. Woodring, *Politics*, p. 46.

30. Coleridge, *Complete Poems*, 2:1144.

31. Coleridge, *Criticism*, p. 253. In this and the next passage Coleridge sets benevolent feeling against intellectual or positive truth, and the source of this distinction, like the talent-genius distinction, may be Coleridge's characterization of Pitt as an effete intellectual who has "no attachment to female society, no fondness for children, no perception of beauty in nature" (*Essays on His Times*, 1:225).

32. Coleridge, *Letters*, 1:244.

33. Coleridge, *Criticism*, p. 321.

34. Coleridge, *Complete Poetical Works*, 1:84.

35. Coleridge, *Letters*, 1:86.

36. Coleridge, *Inquiring Spirit*, p. 80.

37. Coleridge, *Complete Poems*, 2:1136.

38. Coleridge, *Criticism*, pp. 372–73. This last passage obviously bears significantly on Coleridge's own preternatural "Rime of the Ancient Mariner." See also Coleridge's "Apologetic Preface to 'Fire, Famine, and Slaughter,'" in *Complete Poems*, 2:1095–1108.

39. Coleridge, *Inquiring Spirit*, pp. 315–16.

40. Ibid., p. 314.

41. See "Preface to the Second Edition of the *Lyrical Ballads*," in *The Poetical Works of William Wordsworth* (Oxford: Clarendon Press, 1952), 2:386–87.

42. Coleridge, *Letters*, 1:275.

43. Coleridge, *Criticism*, p. 378.

44. Ibid., p. 382.

45. Ibid., p. 370.

46. Colmer, *Coleridge*, p. 39.

47. Coleridge, *Criticism*, pp. 355, 356.

48. Coleridge, *Letters*, 1:354.
49. Coleridge, *Criticism*, p. 374.
50. Ibid., p. 372.
51. Ibid., p. 376.

CHAPTER THREE
Naturalization and Psychology in Coleridge's Shakespeare Criticism, 1800–1812

1. Coleridge, *Shakespeare Criticism*, 2:110. In this chapter, further references are found in the text.
2. MS note reproduced in Coleridge, *Inquiring Spirit*, p. 101.
3. Justifying Edmund's actions in *King Lear*, for example, Coleridge obviously naturalizes him by endowing him with a "powerful intellect" on which certain forces operate to drive him to a course of evil.
4. Culler, *Structuralist Poetics*, p. 237.
5. Allen Tate, "Literature as Knowledge," *Southern Review* 6 (1940–41): 649.
6. M. M. Badawi, *Coleridge: Critic of Shakespeare* (London: Cambridge University Press, 1973).
7. Paul Deschamps, *La Formation de la pensée de Coleridge* (Paris: Didier, 1964), p. 263.
8. Coleridge, *Letters*, 2:706.
9. Both quotations appear in James Volant Baker's *The Sacred River: Coleridge's Theory of the Imagination* (Baton Rouge: Louisiana State University Press, 1957), p. 28.
10. Coleridge, *Table Talk*, 24 June 1827.
11. I. A. Richards, *Coleridge on Imagination* (Bloomington: Indiana University Press, 1960), pp. 67–68.
12. Walter Jackson Bate, *From Classic to Romantic: Premises of Taste in Eighteenth-Century England* (Cambridge: Harvard University Press, 1946), pp. 96–97.
13. Elinor S. Shaffer, "Iago's Malignity Motivated: Coleridge's Unpublished 'Opus Magnum,'" *Shakespeare Quarterly* 19 (1968): 201–2.
14. Ibid., p. 199.
15. Ibid., p. 202.
16. Coleridge, *Notebooks*, vol. 2, no. 2471.

17. Ibid.
18. See Badawi, *Coleridge*, p. 141.
19. S. T. Coleridge, "On the Passions." A transcribed copy of this essay was kindly obtained for me by Professor Ramonda Modiano of the University of Washington. The original is part of the British Museum Manuscript Egerton 2801, 43r–58v. Coleridge's symbol in the note, } {, describes a union of the two words or meanings.
20. Coleridge, *Notebooks*, vol. 2, no. 2086.
21. Coleridge, *Friend*, 1:145.
22. Baker, in *The Sacred River*, chap. 5, for instance.
23. Humphrey House, *Coleridge* (London: Rupert Hart-Davis, 1967), pp. 142–56.
24. Coleridge, *Notebooks*, vol. 2, no. 2012.
25. Ibid., no. 2055.
26. Ibid., no. 2999.
27. Coleridge, *Biographia*, 2:183; idem, *Criticism*, p. 36.
28. Coleridge, *Letters*, 2:864.
29. Coleridge, "On the Passions"; and Dorothy Emmet, "Coleridge on Powers in Mind and Nature," in *Coleridge's Variety*, p. 177.
30. See Elinor S. Shaffer, "Coleridge's Theory of Aesthetic Interest," *Journal of Aesthetics and Art Criticism* 27 (1969): 405.
31. Coleridge, *Biographia*, 2:254.
32. Coleridge, *Notebooks*, vol. 2, no. 2012.
33. Ibid., no. 2112.
34. Coleridge, *Criticism*, p. 190.
35. Coleridge, *Biographia*, 2:51.
36. Coleridge, *Notebooks*, vol. 2, no. 2516.
37. Coleridge, *Criticism*, pp. 356–57. See also idem, *Notebooks*, vol. 1, no. 957.
38. Coleridge, *Notebooks*, vol. 2, no. 2302.
39. Coleridge, *Criticism*, p. 366.
40. Ibid., p. 356.
41. Ibid., pp. 195–96.
42. Coleridge, *Biographia*, 2:67–68.
43. Kenneth Burke's "Psychology and Form," in *Counter-Statement* (Berkeley and Los Angeles: University of California Press, 1931), is a fine illustration of the richness of Coleridge's psychological poetics. Burke uses many of the formal terms I have described in this chapter, and though he is far more cogent and coherent than Coleridge is at times, his debt is obvious.

CHAPTER FOUR
The *Biographia Literaria* and
the Language of Science

1. Coleridge, *Letters*, 4:767.

2. Kathleen Coburn, "Coleridge, a Bridge between Science and Poetry: Reflections on the Bicentenary of His Birth," in *Coleridge's Variety*, pp. 91, 95. My entire chapter is indebted to some suggestions in Coburn's article, and I am more generally indebted to M. H. Abrams's "Coleridge's 'A Light in Sound': Science, Metascience, and Imagination," *Proceedings of the American Philosophical Society* 116 (1972): 458–75.

3. Cited in Alice D. Snyder, *Coleridge on Logic and Learning* (New Haven: Yale University Press, 1929), p. 23.

4. Coleridge, *Treatise on Method*, p. 8.

5. Sir William Lawrence, *Introduction to Comparative Anatomy* (London, 1816), p. 169.

6. Snyder, *Coleridge on Logic*, p. 18.

7. Ibid., p. 21.

8. "Hints towards a More Comprehensive Theory of Life," pp. 405–6. In this chapter, further references are found in the text.

9. Besides the influence of Davy and Abernethy, "Theory of Life" leans heavily on German *Naturphilosophie* and other scientific or pseudoscientific bodies of thought.

10. See David M. Knight, "The Scientist as Sage," *Studies in Romanticism* 6 (1967): 65–88.

11. Coleridge, *Friend*, 1:472.

12. Coleridge, *Letters*, 2:1042.

13. S. H. Davy, *Fragmentary Remains*, ed. John Davy (London: 1858), p. 74.

14. Coleridge, *Letters*, 4:768.

15. Ibid., pp. 758–62.

16. Coleridge, *Friend*, 1:463.

17. Coleridge, *Treatise on Method*, p. 25.

18. Snyder, *Coleridge on Logic*, p. 31.

19. J. R. de J. Jackson, *Method and Imagination in Coleridge's Criticism* (London: Routledge and Kegan Paul, 1969).

20. Coleridge, *Biographia*, 2:65. In this chapter, further references are found in the text.

21. Coleridge, *Shakespearean Criticism*, 2:53. That the language here and at other points in the *Biographia* often comes directly from

Schlegel or Schelling does not weaken my argument, since it is the use of the scientific discourse that matters, not its origin.

22. Isaacs, "Coleridge's Critical Terminology," p. 87.

23. Culler, "Literary History, Allegory, and Semiology," p. 263.

24. Ibid., p. 264.

25. Abrams, *The Mirror and the Lamp*, p. 121.

26. Coleridge, *Criticism*, pp. 95, 42–43.

27. Quoted in Barfield, *What Coleridge Thought*, p. 32.

28. Coleridge, *Letters*, 4:760.

29. Coleridge, *Friend*, 1:478–79.

30. Coleridge, "Genial Criticism," in *Biographia*, 2:235.

31. Coleridge, *Criticism*, 88–89.

32. I. A. Richards, another scientific critic, appropriated this notion from Coleridge.

33. Coleridge, *Criticism*, p. 95.

34. Quoted by Barfield, "Coleridge's Enjoyment of Words," p. 202 (n. 14).

CHAPTER FIVE

Accommodating Aeschylus: Coleridge, Theology, and Literary Criticism

1. Two contemporary readings of this lecture are George Whalley's "Coleridge on the *Prometheus* of Aeschylus" in *Transactions of the Royal Society of Canada*, 3d ser., 54 (1960): 13–24; and chap. 7 of Jackson's *Method and Imagination*.

2. Coleridge, *Letters*, 5:461.

3. Coleridge, *Criticism*, p. 170. In this chapter, further references are in the text.

4. J. Robert Barth, S.J., *Coleridge and Christian Doctrine* (Cambridge: Harvard University Press, 1969), p. viii.

5. "Limbo," "Ne Plus Ultra," and several other poems written when Coleridge entered this last period of his life are indeed often as agonized as his earlier poems. Yet, even in these instances, the questions and conflicts appear in a chiefly theological form, and the arguments, however unorthodox from one point of view, remain frequently in the framework of traditional religious experience.

6. Barth points out that the principles of Coleridge's approach to the Scriptures were three: "(1) the distinction between inspira-

tion and revelation; (2) the unique instrumentality of the inspired author of Scripture; and (3) the special nature of scriptural inerrancy" (*Coleridge and Christian Doctrine*, pp. 59–60). Elinor S. Shaffer has also discussed this question at various points in *"Kubla Khan" and the Fall of Jerusalem* (Cambridge: Cambridge University Press, 1975).

7. Coleridge, *Confessions of an Inquiring Spirit*, ed. Henry Nelson Coleridge (London: William Pickering, 1840), p. 9–10. In this chapter, further references are in the text.

8. Dante and Saint Thomas Aquinas are perhaps the most famous proponents of this kind of interpretive process.

9. See Barth, *Coleridge and Christian Doctrine*, pp. 71–73.

10. Notebook 54, f. [19v]. Quoted in Barth, *Coleridge and Christian Docrtine*, pp. 73–74.

11. Coleridge, *Aids to Reflection*, p. 43.

12. John Tulloch, "Coleridge and His School," in *Movements of Religious Thought in Britain during the Nineteenth Century*, St. Giles Lectures (London: no imprint, 1885), p. 25.

13. In *Church and State*, Coleridge himself calls his description and arguments "models."

14. "Essay on Faith," in *The Literary Remains of Samuel Taylor Coleridge*, ed. Henry Nelson Coleridge (London: William Pickering, 1839), 4:438.

15. Ibid., 3:403–4.

16. See also Coleridge's *Confessions*, pp. 73–78; and idem, "Definition of a Miracle," in *Literary Remains*, 1:370–72.

17. Coleridge, *Literary Remains*, 3:391–92.

18. Ibid., p. 392.

19. Ibid., p. 407.

20. Ibid., pp. 399–400.

21. Coleridge, *Church and State*, pp. 24, 29.

22. Coleridge, "On the *Prometheus* of Aeschylus," in *Literary Remains*, 2:323. In this chapter, further references are found in the text.

23. Coleridge, *Aids to Reflection*, pp. 232–33.

24. Coleridge, *Philosophical Lectures*, p. 112.

25. Barfield, *What Coleridge Thought*, p. 165.

26. Coleridge, *Philosophical Lectures*, pp. 111–12. See also idem, *Friend*, 1:505–6.

27. Coleridge, *Table Talk*, 8 May 1824.

28. Coleridge, *Table Talk*, 9 July 1832.

29. Coleridge, *Church and State*, p. 233. Coleridge does not print it exactly in this form.

30. For example, when Coleridge objects to a phrase in Scott's *Old Mortality*, which claims feeling rather than reason as a basis for Christian faith, his objection follows from an important distinction between the theological significance of the two words. He says it is "not the feelings of *natural* humanity" which lead to faith, "but the principles of immutable reason" (*Criticism*, p. 326).

CONCLUSION
The Tangential Critic

1. William Rueckert, "Literary Criticism and History: The Endless Dialectic," *New Literary History* 6 (1975): 496.

2. *The Complete Works of William Hazlitt*, ed. P. P. Howe (London and Toronto: J. M. Dent, 1932), 2:29.

3. Coleridge, *Aids to Reflection*, p. xlviii.

Bibliography

Abrams, M. H. "Coleridge's 'A Light in Sound': Science, Metascience, and Imagination." *Proceedings of the American Philosophical Society* 116 (1972): 458–75.

——. *The Mirror and the Lamp.* New York: Oxford University Press, 1953.

Badawi, M. M. *Coleridge: Critic of Shakespeare.* London: Cambridge University Press, 1973.

Baker, James. *The Sacred River: Coleridge's Theory of the Imagination.* Baton Rouge: Louisiana State University Press, 1957.

Barfield, Owen. "Coleridge's Enjoyment of Words." In *Coleridge's Variety.* Edited by John Beer. Pittsburgh: University of Pittsburgh Press, 1975, pp. 204–19.

——. *What Coleridge Thought.* Middletown, Conn.: Wesleyan University Press, 1971.

Barth, J. Robert, S.J. *Coleridge and Christian Doctrine.* Cambridge: Harvard University Press, 1969.

Barthes, Roland. *S/Z.* New York: Hill and Wang, 1974.

Bate, Walter Jackson. *From Classic to Romantic: Premises of Taste in Eighteenth-Century England.* Cambridge: Harvard University Press, 1946.

Burke, Kenneth. *Counter-Statement.* Berkeley and Los Angeles: University of California Press, 1931.

Cobban, Alfred. *Edmund Burke and the Revolt against the Eighteenth Century.* Northampton: John Dickens and Co., 1929.

Coburn, Kathleen. "Coleridge, a Bridge between Science and Poetry: Reflections on the Bicentenary of His Birth." In *Coleridge's Variety.* Edited by John Beer. Pittsburgh: University of Pittsburgh Press, 1975, pp. 81–100.

Coleridge, Samuel Taylor. *Aids to Reflection.* Edited by Henry Nelson Coleridge. New York: William Gowans, 1863.

——. *Biographia Literaria.* Edited with "Aesthetical Essays" by J. Shawcross. 2 vols. Oxford: Oxford University Press, 1907.

211

———. *Collected Letters of Samuel Taylor Coleridge*. Edited by E. L. Griggs. 6 vols. London: Oxford University Press, 1956–71.
———. *The Complete Poetical Works of Samuel Taylor Coleridge*. Edited by Ernest Hartley Coleridge. 2 vols. London: Oxford University Press, 1912.
———. *The Complete Works of Samuel Taylor Coleridge*. Edited by W. G. T. Shedd. 7 vols. New York: Harper Brothers, 1958.
———. *Confessions of an Inquiring Spirit*. Edited by Henry Nelson Coleridge. London: William Pickering, 1840.
———. *Essays on His Times*. Edited by David Erdman. Princeton, N.J.: Princeton University Press, 1978.
———. *The Friend*. Edited by Barbara E. Rooke. 2 vols. London: Routledge and Kegan Paul, 1969.
———. *Inquiring Spirit: A New Presentation of Coleridge from His Published and Unpublished Prose Writings*. Edited by Kathleen Coburn. New York: Minerva Press, 1951.
———. *Lay Sermons*. Edited by R. J. White. London: Routledge and Kegan Paul, 1972.
———. *Lectures 1795 on Politics and Religion*. Edited by Lewis Patton and Peter Mann. London: Routledge and Kegan Paul, 1971.
———. *The Literary Remains of Samuel Taylor Coleridge*. Edited by Henry Nelson Coleridge. London: William Pickering, 1836–39.
———. *Miscellaneous Criticism*. Edited by T. M. Raysor. Cambridge: Harvard University Press, 1936.
———. *Miscellanies, Aesthetic and Literary*. Edited by T. Ashe. London: G. Bell, 1911.
———. *The Notebooks of Samuel Taylor Coleridge*. Edited by Kathleen Coburn. 3 (of 6) vols. London and New York: Pantheon Books, 1957–.
———. *On the Constitution of Church and State*. Edited by John Colmer. London: Routledge and Kegan Paul, 1976.
———. *The Philosophical Lectures*. Edited by Kathleen Coburn. New York: Philosophical Library, 1949.
———. *S. T. Coleridge's Treatise on Method*. Edited by Alice D. Snyder. London: Constable and Co., 1934.
———. *Shakespearean Criticism*. Edited by T. M. Raysor. 2 vols. London: Dent and Sons, 1960.
———. *The Watchman*. Edited by Lewis Patton. London: Routledge and Kegan Paul, 1970.

Colmer, John. *Coleridge: Critic of Society.* London: Oxford University Press, 1959.

Culler, Jonathan. "Literary History, Allegory, and Semiology." *New Literary History* 7 (1976): 259–71.

———. *Structuralist Poetics.* Ithaca, N.Y.: Cornell University Press, 1975.

Davy, Humphry. *Fragmentary Remains.* Edited by John Davy. London, 1858.

Derrida, Jacques. "Structure, Sign, and Play in the Discourse of the Human Sciences." In *The Structuralist Controversy: The Languages of Criticism and the Sciences of Man.* Edited by Richard Macksey and Eugenio Donato. Baltimore: Johns Hopkins University Press, 1970, pp. 247–65.

Deschamps, Paul. *La Formation de la pensée de Coleridge.* Paris: Didier, 1964.

Emmet, Dorothy. "Coleridge on Powers in Mind and Nature." In *Coleridge's Variety.* Edited by John Beer. Pittsburgh: University of Pittsburgh Press, 1975, pp. 166–83.

Haven, Richard. *Patterns of Consciousness.* Amherst: University of Massachusetts Press, 1969.

Hyman, Stanley Edgar. *The Armed Vision.* New York: Knopf, 1948.

Isaacs, J. "Coleridge's Critical Terminology." *Essays and Studies* 21 (1936): 86–105.

Iser, Wolfgang. "The Reading Process: A Phenomenological Approach." In *New Directions in Literary History.* Edited by Ralph Cohen. Baltimore: Johns Hopkins University Press, 1974.

Jackson, J. R. de J. *Method and Imagination in Coleridge's Criticism.* London: Routledge and Kegan Paul, 1969.

Jakobson, Roman. "On Linguistic Aspects of Translation." *Selected Writings.* Vol. 2. The Hague: Mouton, 1971.

Knight, David M. "The Scientist as Sage." *Studies in Romanticism* 6 (1967): 65–88.

Lawrence, Sir William. *Introduction to Comparative Anatomy.* 1816.

Richards, I. A. *Coleridge on Imagination.* Bloomington: Indiana University Press, 1960.

Rueckert, William. "Literary Criticism and History: The Endless Dialectic." *New Literary History* 6 (1975): 491–512.

Sankey, Benjamin T. "Coleridge on Milton's Satan." *Philological Quarterly* 41 (1962): 504–5.

Shaffer, Elinor S. "Coleridge's Theory of Aesthetic Interest." *Journal of Aesthetics and Art Criticism* 27 (1969): 392–406.

———. "Iago's Malignity Motivated: Coleridge's Unpublished 'Opus Magnum.'" *Shakespeare Quarterly* 19 (1968): 195–203.

———. *"Kubla Khan" and The Fall of Jerusalem.* Cambridge: Cambridge University Press, 1975.

Snyder, Alice D. *Coleridge on Logic and Learning.* New Haven: Yale University Press, 1929.

Sollers, Philipe. *Logiques.* Paris: Seuil, 1968.

Southey, Robert. *The Life of Wesley.* 2 vols. London: Oxford University Press, 1925.

Steiner, George. *After Babel.* London: Oxford University Press, 1975.

———. "Whorf, Chomsky, and the Student of Literature." *New Literary History* 4 (1972): 15–34.

Tate, Allen. "Literature as Knowledge." *Southern Review* 6 (1940–41): 640–55.

Tulloch, John. "Coleridge and His School." In *Movements of Religious Thought in Britain during the Nineteenth Century.* St. Giles Lectures. London, 1885.

Whalley, George. "Coleridge on the *Prometheus* of Aeschylus." *Transactions of the Royal Society of Canada,* 3d ser., 54 (1960): 13–24.

Woodring, Carl. *Politics in the Poetry of Coleridge.* Madison: University of Wisconsin Press, 1961.

Wordsworth, William. "Preface to the Second Edition of the *Lyrical Ballads.*" In *The Poetical Works of William Wordsworth.* Vol. 2. Oxford: Clarendon Press, 1952.

Index